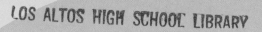
ARE YOU "NORMAL"?

BY MARK SHULMAN

NATIONAL GEOGRAPHIC

WASHINGTON, D.C.

PUBLISHED BY THE
NATIONAL GEOGRAPHIC SOCIETY
John M. Fahey, Jr., *Chairman of the Board and Chief Executive Officer*
Timothy T. Kelly, *President*
Declan Moore, *Executive Vice President; President, Publishing*
Melina Gerosa Bellows, *Chief Creative Officer, Kids and Family, Global Media*

Prepared by the Book Division
Nancy Laties Feresten, *Senior Vice President, Editor in Chief, Children's Books*
Jonathan Halling, *Design Director, Children's Publishing*
Jennifer Emmett, *Editorial Director, Children's Books*
Jay Sumner, *Director of Photography, Children's Publishing*
Carl Mehler, *Director of Maps*
R. Gary Colbert, *Production Director*
Jennifer A. Thornton, *Managing Editor*

Staff for This Book
Becky Baines, *Project Editor*
Eva Absher, *Art Director/Designer*
Lori Epstein, *Senior Illustrations Editor*
Kate Olesin, *Editorial Assistant*
Kathryn Robbins, *Design Production Assistant*
Hillary Moloney, *Illustrations Assistant*
Grace Hill, *Associate Managing Editor*
Joan Gossett, *Production Editor*
Chelsea Zillmer, *Researcher*
Lewis R. Bassford, *Production Manager*
Susan Borke, *Legal and Business Affairs*

Manufacturing and Quality Management
Christopher A. Liedel, *Chief Financial Officer*
Phillip L. Schlosser, *Senior Vice President*
Chris Brown, *Technical Director*
Nicole Elliott, *Manager*
Rachel Faulise, *Manager*
Robert L. Barr, *Manager*

Printed in China

11/PPS/1

 The National Geographic Society is one of the world's largest nonprofit scientific and educational organizations. Founded in 1888 to "increase and diffuse geographic knowledge," the Society works to inspire people to care about the planet. National Geographic reflects the world through its magazines, television programs, films, music and radio, books, DVDs, maps, exhibitions, live events, school publishing programs, interactive media, and merchandise. *National Geographic* magazine, the Society's official journal, published in English and 33 local-language editions, is read by more than 38 million people each month. The National Geographic Channel reaches 320 million households in 34 languages in 166 countries. National Geographic Digital Media receives more than 15 million visitors a month. National Geographic has funded more than 9,400 scientific research, conservation and exploration projects and supports an education program promoting geography literacy. For more information, visit nationalgeographic.com.

For more information, please call 1-800-NGS LINE (647-5463) or write to the following address:
National Geographic Society
1145 17th Street N.W.
Washington, DC 20036-4688 U.S.A.

Visit us online at
www.nationalgeographic.com/books

For librarians and teachers:
www.ngchildrensbooks.org

More for kids from National Geographic:
kids.nationalgeographic.com

For information about special discounts for bulk purchases, please contact National Geographic Books Special Sales:
ngspecsales@ngs.org

For rights or permissions inquiries, please contact National Geographic Books
Subsidiary Rights: ngbookrights@ngs.org

CON-TENTS

ARE YOU "NORMAL?"

ARE YOU "NORMAL"?

WELL, ARE YOU?

IT ALL DEPENDS ON HOW YOU LOOK AT THINGS.

If you bite your fingernails, you're normal. But if you bite your toenails, you're not. So, what happens if you bite them both? Are you normal?

NORMAL

CHANGES FROM PLACE TO PLACE.

Wear a furry parka in July and you're normal . . . in Antarctica. Gobble up pickled vegetables and raw eggs for breakfast and you're normal . . . in Japan. Walk to school every day and you're normal . . . in New York City. So, are you normal?

YES. AND NO.

We scoured the Internet for weeks looking for questions kids had been asked about everyday life. Thousands of kids were surveyed. Dozens of calculators were harmed in the process. The incredible results packed inside this colorful, fun, and informative book come from the answers kids gave. Are the answers facts? Some are, but most of them are opinions. Opinions change all the time. And they're every bit as fascinating as the kids who have them.

WHO ANSWERED THESE QUESTIONS?

For some of these questions, National Geographic polled its amazing readers across the United States and Canada. For other questions, we used surveys from a number of sources (all of which can be found at the back of the book).

What did we find? Some of these questions may prove you're totally "normal." Others may prove you're totally "weird." But mix all 100+ questions together and you'll discover one undeniable fact:

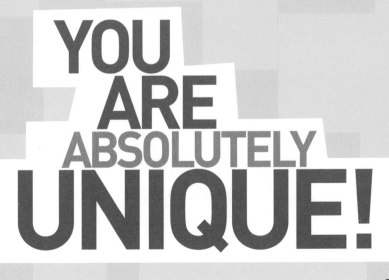

YOU ARE ABSOLUTELY UNIQUE!

ABOUT THE NUMBERS

HOW DO I USE THE BOOK?

1 READ THE QUESTIONS

2 ANSWER THE QUESTIONS

3 TOTAL UP YOUR WEIRD-O-METER POINTS FOR EACH CHAPTER

4 LOWER NUMBERS = NORMAL
HIGHER NUMBERS = NOT SO NORMAL

5 GET DIFFERENT RESULTS FOR EACH CHAPTER

6 IT'S COMPLETELY NORMAL TO HAVE FUN

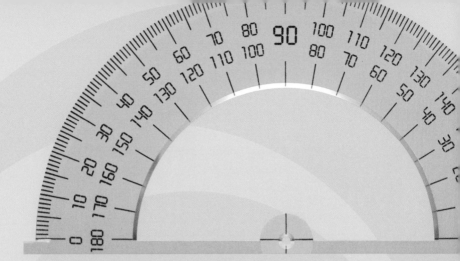

WHAT DO THESE NUMBERS MEAN?

Your answer to each question will be assigned Weird-O-Meter points located at the bottom of each page. Keep track of your score as you go through the chapter, so you can determine your overall Weird-O-Meter ranking for each section. The numbers range 1-4, so even if your answer is totally out there, and only 2 out of 100 kids answered the same way, the highest you can get is 4 points. That way, one super-strange (or super-normal) answer won't totally throw off your number.

WHERE DO I FIND OUT HOW NORMAL I AM?

At the end of each section, you'll total up your points to see how normal (or weird) you are compared with all the other kids.

You might find you're totally weird in one category and totally normal in another. Or you might be about the same from category to category but vary a lot from question to question. Any way you score is totally your own and totally fine.

(MORE)
ABOUT THE
NUMBERS

WHEN WILL THESE NUMBERS MAKE SENSE?

You may not have learned fractions or percentages yet. But don't worry, it's not so hard. Imagine 10 kids in a row. If 5 of them agree on the same answer, then that's the same as writing "half the kids agree" or "5 out of 10 agree" or "1/2 agree" or "50% agree."

A PERCENT EQUALS 1 PART OF 100.
So, 50 parts of 100 = 50 percent = 50% = 50/100 = 1/2 = 50 people out of every 100. The lower the percent, the less normal something is. If 97% of your friends wear pants on their legs, it's super normal. If 3% wear them on their heads, it's really, really NOT normal.

really normal **97%**   **3%** really not normal

So, if ten thousand kids answer a question, and five thousand kids answer the same way, then that's the same as half, or 1/2, or 50%, or... you get the idea.

HERE'S A CHART. SEE IF YOU CAN SPOT THE PATTERNS.

HOW MANY KIDS ANSWERED THE SAME WAY?	AS WORDS	AS A PERCENT
Half 1/2	5 out of 10	50%
A third 1/3	About 3 out of 10 or 1 out of 3	About 33%
A fourth or a quarter 1/4	1 out of 4	25%
A fifth 1/5	2 out of 10 or 1 out of 5	20%
A sixth 1/6	1 out of 6	About 17%
A seventh 1/7	1 out of 7	About 15%
An eighth 1/8	1 out of 8	About 12%
A ninth 1/9	1 out of 9	About 11%
A tenth 1/10	1 out of 10	10%

ABOUT POLLS The kids who answered the questions are from the United States and Canada and are within a few years of your age. Like all polls, these results represent the opinions of the people surveyed. The people who answer are called a sample. If a sample is big enough and similar enough to the population in general, then it can show the breakdown of what the larger population thinks at a particular time. If a sample is not large enough, or not assembled scientifically, then it is not always a good indicator of everyone's opinion. People can also answer questions differently depending on how the questions are asked. These different factors can lead to different results. So polls are useful tools for finding out what people think, but they are not perfect. Try asking your friends or family or class these questions and you'll see that your poll gets slightly different results.

You might notice that if you add up the percentages in each answer, some are slightly above or below 100%. That's because in some cases the original data was rounded up or down. The results will still give you an idea of the bigger picture. The data collected for this book is up to date as of May 2011.

ARE YOU "NORMAL"?

HOME

HOME QUIZ

BE SURE TO
KEEP TRACK OF
YOUR ANSWERS!

1 GOT PETS?
- Yes
- No

2 HOW MANY, IF ANY?
- 1
- 2
- 3
- 4
- 5+

3 WHICH CHORE DO YOU HATE HATE HATE THE MOST MOST MOST?
- Cleaning my room!
- Doing the dishes!
- Laundry work!
- Making beds!
- Setting the table!
- Sweeping and mopping!

4 TOP FAVORITE PET?
- Dog
- Cat
- Hamster
- Rabbit
- Fish

14

5 DO YOU MAKE YOUR BED EVERY DAY?
- Yes
- No

6 HOW MUCH TELEVISION DO YOU *REALLY* WATCH EACH DAY?
- None
- Less than 1 hour
- 1-2 hours
- 2-3 hours
- More than 3 hours

7 WHAT KIND OF HOUSE IS HOME?
- House
- Apartment
- Neither
- Both

8 DO YOU HAVE A T.V. IN YOUR BEDROOM?
- Yes
- No

9 YOUR OWN BEDROOM?
- Yes
- No
- Sometimes

10 YOUR OWN BATHROOM?
- Yes
- No

15

1 GOT PETS?

YES
You're in good company. 6 out of 10 households have a pet.

NO
Don't have a pet? Don't sweat. 4 out of 10 households don't either.

WEIRD-O-METER YES = 2, NO = 3

2 HOW MANY, IF ANY?

1 pet? So do 73% of kids.

2 pets? 16% of kids agree.

3 pets? Very few kids—about 6%—have 3 pets.

4 pets? You're far from normal. Just among the 2.5% of 4-pet owners, in fact.

5+ pets? Still weird. Only another 2.5% could open their own zoo.

WEIRD-O-METER 1 PET = 1, 2 PETS = 3, ANYTHING ELSE = 4. IF YOU HAVE NO PETS, SCORE YOURSELF A 2!

3 WHICH CHORE DO YOU HATE HATE HATE THE MOST MOST MOST?

- If cleaning your room makes you wish you had a dentist appointment instead, you're as normal as stuffing things under the bed. Over half of kids prefer clutter to clean.

- What's something you love to eat on and hate to wash? Did you say dishes? Oh, you heard that one before! So did 1 in 5 kids.

- Here's one that will floor you: 1 in 9 kids hates sweeping and mopping.

- Want the cold, wet facts? 1 in 12 kids can't stand laundry day.

- You lie in your bed. Now make it! No? Then you're the 1 out of 25 kids who says it's your worst chore.

- Are you happy to hear that the dish ran away with the spoon? That makes you the 1 in 50 kids who doesn't like setting the table.

WEIRD-O-METER CLEAN ROOM = 2, DISHES = 2, SWEEP/MOP = 3, ANYTHING ELSE = 4

4 TOP FAVORITE PET?

DID YOU SAY DOG?
Over half of all kids made man's best friend the most normal answer in the end.

COULD IT BE CAT?
1 in 6 kids likes a feline just fine.

HAVE TO HAVE A HAMSTER?
1 in 9 likes pets on a wheel.

REALLY LIKE A RABBIT?
1 in 11 agrees, these furry pets are fur me!

FAVORITE IS FISH?
1 in 20 likes fish plenty.

WEIRD-**O**-METER DOG = 1, CAT = 3, HAMSTER = 3, ANYTHING ELSE = 4

5 DO YOU MAKE YOUR BED EVERY DAY?

NO! You can't make me make it! If this is your position, 4 out of 5 kids are on your team.

YES! 1 in 5 kids smooths out the covers every day. Isn't that neat?

WEIRD-**O**-METER   NO = 1, YES = 4

6 HOW MUCH TELEVISION DO YOU *REALLY* WATCH EACH DAY?

NONE?
Not normal. Only 9% of kids spend all their time in the real world.

LESS THAN 1 HOUR?
25% of the kids turn on, tune in, and then drop out in 60 minutes or less.

1-2 HOURS?
That's the most normal. 44% of your peers peer at the TV for that long.

MORE THAN 3 HOURS?
7% of kids can't get enough TV, no matter how hard they try!

2-3 HOURS?
15% of kids put that much TV on the daily menu.

WEIRD-**O**-METER   NONE = 4, LESS THAN 1 HOUR = 2, 1-2 HOURS = 2, 2-3 HOURS = 3, OVER 3 HOURS = 4

7 WHAT KIND OF HOUSE IS HOME?

WHAT MAKES A HOME A HOUSE? 19 out of 25 kids know the answer: A triangle roof, a snake of smoke coming up from the chimney, and the fact that they live in it.

4 out of 25 kids call an apartment home. Some of them even get to ride an elevator every day . . . unless there's a power blackout. Then they walk up 10 floors.

1 in 25 says they've got an apartment and a house. And another 1 in 25 says they don't live in either.

But we didn't ask about igloos, yurts, log cabins, or tree houses!

WEIRD-O-METER   HOUSE = 1, APARTMENT = 3, ANYTHING ELSE = 4

8

CAN U.C. A T.V. IN B.E.D.?

◗ Just over half of kids (56%) practice the 3 R's:
Recline (in bed)
Remote (control)
Retire (eventually)

◗ The other almost-half (44%) have to step out to tune in . . . step out of the bedroom, that is.

WEIRD-O-METER YES = 2, NO = 3

9 YOUR OWN BEDROOM?

NO

It's raining! It's pouring!
Your brother or sister is snoring!
Take the pillow from your bed,
Toss it onto his or her head
And hope you can sleep until morning!
(And by the way, just over half the kids share a room.)

YES

Aren't you just the tiniest bit lonely? No? We didn't think so. 1 out of 3 kids has their own room. Keep out!

SOMETIMES

Depending on your point of view, these sometimes sharers are sometimes lucky. But which times are the lucky times? That's up to you. 1 out of 6 mixes it up.

WEIRD-O-METER   NO = 2, YES = 3, SOMETIMES = 3

10 YOUR OWN BATHROOM?

NO. Hate to wait when you just can't wait? When you gotta go, you gotta go in the family bathroom. But don't sweat it: 6 out of 10 kids are in the same, long line every morning.

YES. When you know you've got to go, do you get to take it easy? If you can have all the time in the world in your own bathroom, 4 out of 10 kids are standing there with you. Well, not literally.

WEIRD-O-METER NO = 2, YES = 3

WHERE ARE YOU ON THE WEIRD-O-METER?

ADD UP YOUR SCORE AND YOU'LL GET A WEIRDNESS NUMBER YOU CAN TAKE **HOME.**

0-22

YOU'RE AS NORMAL AS LIVING IN A HOUSE.

For you, home is the kind of place that's familiar to a lot of families. Odds are, you've got a house, a pet, a TV, and maybe even a kitchen and bed . . . but the thought of making it makes you wish you didn't.

0

10

23-29

YOU'RE AS NORMAL AS LIVING IN A BOAT.

How's your house? For one thing, it's a little bit different than the average. For another, you've probably got some interesting things stowed away in there. Maybe not a crazy wild pet, but possibly a gerbil? Chances are, you have a nice clean room and a well-made bed because it's normal not to.

30-40

YOU'RE AS NORMAL AS LIVING IN A BLIMP.

Home, home on the strange . . . What goes with an address like yours? Maybe a dog, 2 cats, a couple of snakes, and a Bengal tiger. What's the hardest part of having such a not-so-normal house? Where to keep the tiger, of course. Wherever you live, your friends probably come over and find something pretty cool.

20   30   40

ARE YOU "NORMAL"?

SCHOOL

SCHOOL QUIZ

BE SURE TO KEEP TRACK OF YOUR ANSWERS!

1 WHAT DO YOU LIKE BEST ABOUT SCHOOL?
- Hanging out with friends
- My teacher
- Recess
- Lunch
- Actually learning something
- Nothing

2 SERIOUSLY, WHAT'S YOUR BEST SUBJECT?
- Math
- Science
- Reading
- Writing
- History

3 WEAR A SCHOOL UNIFORM?
- Yes
- No

4 NAME YOUR FAVORITE SCHOOL UNIFORM COLOR.
- Black
- Green
- Blue
- Red
- White
- Other

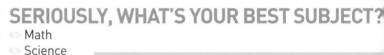

5 EVER REPEAT A GRADE?

- Yes
- No

6 HOMEWORK? HOW MANY HOURS A WEEK DO YOU DONATE TO THE CAUSE?

- Less than 1 hour
- 1-2 hours
- 3-5 hours
- 6-8 hours
- 9-11 hours
- 12 or more hours

7 HOW DO YOU GET TO SCHOOL IN THE MORNING?

- Walk
- Bicycle
- Bus
- Car
- Train
- Other

8 SCHOOL BUS! WHERE DO YOU SIT?

- Front
- Middle
- Back
- It doesn't matter

9 YOU MISSED *HOW* MANY SCHOOL DAYS LAST YEAR?

- 0
- 1-5
- 6-10
- 11-15
- 16-20
- More than 20

10 WHAT IS THE ABSOLUTELY TOTALLY VERY FIRST THING YOU DO AFTER SCHOOL?

- Play outside
- Play video games
- Watch TV
- Have a snack
- Do homework

1

WHAT DO YOU LIKE BEST ABOUT SCHOOL?

The main reason HALF of all kids like school? Friends, duh!

Teachers are the second biggest, with 1 in 7 kids raising their hand for that answer.

Out of every 9 kids, 1 is there to actually learn something!

Only 1 in 12 is there for recess. Probably because a lot of schools don't have recess anymore.

Only 1 in 14 is in school for the great gourmet lunch cuisine.

And a whopping 1 out of 8 kids likes nothing best about school. Surprised?

WEIRD-O-METER FRIENDS = 2, LUNCH = 4, ANYTHING ELSE = 3

2 SERIOUSLY, WHAT'S YOUR BEST SUBJECT?

With 1 out of 3, it all adds up to math being the top pick.

Science is subject number two. 1 out of 5 kids prefers serious science (like what they serve in the cafeteria).

Enjoy reading about reading? Read on! 1 out of 6 will too.

1 out of 6 kids wishes history would repeat itself. Over and over and over.

If writing is more your type, 1 in 7 agrees.

WEIRD-**O**-METER   MATH = 2, SCIENCE = 2, ANYTHING ELSE = 3

3 WEAR A SCHOOL UNIFORM?

NO!
4 out of 5 kids get to wear whatever they want to school, just as long as their parents let them leave the house.

YES!
1 out of 5 kids wears a uniform. Don't worry, so does Superman.

WEIRD-O-METER   NO = 1, YES = 4

4 NAME YOUR FAVORITE SCHOOL UNIFORM COLOR.

THE PEOPLE HAVE SPOKEN!
BLACK IS GREAT AT SCHOOL
(especially ninja school).

HERE'S THE BREAKDOWN:

BLACK: 1 out of 3 agrees.

BLUE: 1 out of 4 likes it more.

OTHER: 1 out of 6 prefers a mix.

GREEN: 1 out of 8 says it's great.

WHITE: 1 out of 12 thinks it's swell.

RED: 1 out of 14 thinks red is their scene.

WEIRD-**O**-METER   BLACK = 2, BLUE = 2, OTHER = 2,
GREEN = 3, WHITE = 3, RED = 4

5 EVER REPEAT REPEAT REPEAT A GRADE?

🕐 A number of kids—1 out of 10—said yes, yes, I repeated a grade.

⬤ And almost 9 out of 10 said no, once was definitely enough!

WEIRD-O-METER NO = 1, YES = 4

6 HOMEWORK? HOW MANY HOURS OF THE WEEK DO YOU DONATE TO THE CAUSE?

1 out of 3 takes under an hour to do the week's homework.

1 out of 4 hits the books for an hour or two each week.

1 out of 6 studies for 3-5 hours.

1 out of 14 studies and studies for 6-8 hours.

1 out of 25 studies, studies, studies for 9-11 hours.

1 out of 9 kids spends 12+ hours a week on homework. That's about 2 hours a day. Now you know who's going to be your doctor some day!

WEIRD-O-METER LESS THAN 1 = 2, 1-2 = 2, 3-5 = 2, 6-8 = 4, 9-11 = 4, 12+ = 3

7 HOW DO YOU GET TO SCHOOL IN THE MORNING?

39% say they hitch a ride in a car, making it the most normal answer.

35% City bus? Yellow bus? Doesn't matter.

14% walk (so they can tell their grandkids they did).

2% use pedal power.

2% train it.

5% go a different way entirely. Helicopter? Elephant? Submarine? Whatever it is, it's probably cool.

WEIRD-O-METER CAR = 2, BUS = 2, WALK = 3, ANYTHING ELSE = 4

8 SCHOOL BUS!
WHERE DO YOU SIT?

22% sit up near the driver.

13% sit in the middle.

47% sit in the back (where they won't get caught?).

17% say it doesn't matter (as long as they're sitting down).

WITH SO MANY KIDS IN THE BACK, THE BUS SHOULD BE DOING WHEELIES!

WEIRD-O-METER BACK = 2, ANYTHING ELSE = 3. IF YOU DON'T RIDE THE BUS SCORE YOURSELF 2!

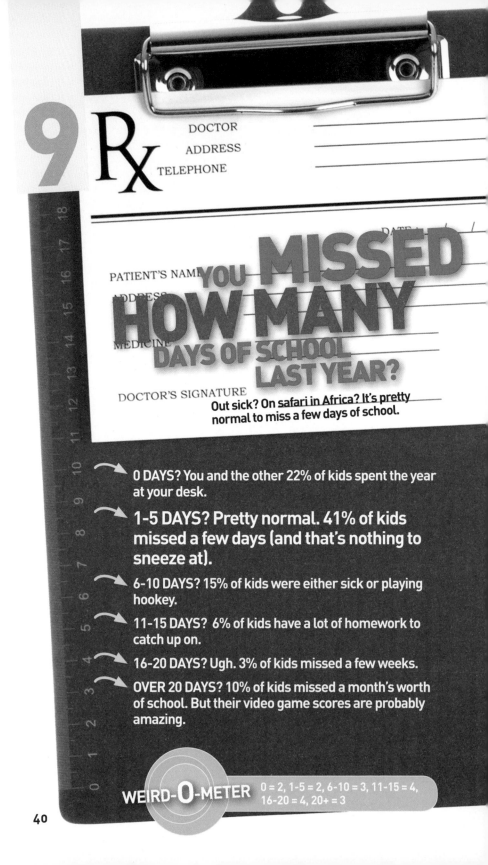

9

R_X

DOCTOR

ADDRESS

TELEPHONE

DATE / /

PATIENT'S NAME

ADDRESS

MEDICINE

DOCTOR'S SIGNATURE

YOU MISSED HOW MANY DAYS OF SCHOOL LAST YEAR?

Out sick? On safari in Africa? It's pretty normal to miss a few days of school.

0 DAYS? You and the other 22% of kids spent the year at your desk.

1-5 DAYS? Pretty normal. 41% of kids missed a few days (and that's nothing to sneeze at).

6-10 DAYS? 15% of kids were either sick or playing hookey.

11-15 DAYS? 6% of kids have a lot of homework to catch up on.

16-20 DAYS? Ugh. 3% of kids missed a few weeks.

OVER 20 DAYS? 10% of kids missed a month's worth of school. But their video game scores are probably amazing.

WEIRD-**O**-METER 0 = 2, 1-5 = 2, 6-10 = 3, 11-15 = 4, 16-20 = 4, 20+ = 3

10 WHAT IS THE ABSOLUTELY TOTALLY VERY FIRST THING YOU DO AFTER SCHOOL?

SNACK ATTACK?

Almost 1 out of 3 hungry humans eats a snack as soon as they can.

RATHER PLAY THE TV THAN WATCH IT? Video games score with a fifth of the just-got-homers.

TV TIME? A quarter of kids unwind in front of the tube.

HIT THE BOOKS? Wait . . . you actually sit down . . . open a book . . . and do homework first? You're not as weird as you might think. So do a fifth of your friends.

HEARING THE CALL OF THE WILD? That's natural, but only 1 in 12 kids plays outdoors first.

WEIRD-O-METER SNACK = 2, TV = 2, VIDEO GAMES = 3, HOMEWORK = 3, PLAY OUTSIDE = 4

WHERE ARE YOU ON THE WEIRD-O-METER?

ADD UP YOUR SCORE AND YOU'LL GET A WEIRDNESS NUMBER YOU CAN TAKE TO SCHOOL.

1-24

YOU'RE AS NORMAL AS SAYING "I FORGOT MY HOMEWORK."

For you, school is probably not just a place to learn, but one-stop shopping where you can find all your friends. You probably don't wear a uniform, unless you count a thousand kids wearing jeans. How do you know it's a thousand? Because math is likely your favorite subject. When it comes to school, you go with the flow and you like it that way.

YOU'RE AS NORMAL AS SAYING "MY DOG ATE MY HOMEWORK."

While everyone else is learning the recorder, you occasionally bust out the trumpet. And independent assignments are where you really make the grade. When you're supposed to use a #2 pencil, you sometimes use a #3. Because you like to mix it up.

YOU'RE AS NORMAL AS SAYING "MY DOG ATE MY COMPUTER."

How do you get to school? Well, if you could hang-glide in before the bell, you certainly would. You might wear a uniform, but if you do, you've figured out some way to personalize it. And when it's time to make a diorama, you probably use a refrigerator box. That's because you're on the cutting edge.

20

30

40

ARE YOU "NORMAL"?

FRIENDS

FRIENDS QUIZ

BE SURE TO KEEP TRACK OF YOUR ANSWERS!

1 HOW OFTEN EACH WEEK DO YOU HANG OUT WITH ANY FRIENDS ANYWHERE?

- 1 or 2 times a week
- 3 or 4 times a week
- Between 5 days and EVERY day!

2 WHAT ABOUT THE NEIGHBORHOOD KIDS?

- 5 or more days a week
- 3 or 4 days a week
- 1 or 2 days a week
- 0 days a week

3 WHERE DO YOU AND YOUR PALS HANG OUT?

- Your house
- A friend's house
- The mall
- A sports field/court/rink
- A park
- A restaurant
- The pool or beach
- Anywhere your friends are
- None of the above

4 PICK ONE: A FEW BEST FRIENDS OR LOTS OF ACQUAINTANCES?
- One or two really close friends
- Tons of acquaintances

5 WHAT'S THE TOP TOPIC WITH YOUR FRIENDS?
- Something new going on
- Someone we're crushing on
- Fashion and clothes
- People who aren't there to hear!

6 BEEN "DUMPED" BY A FRIEND?
- You bet!
- Not yet!

7 GOT A CRUSH ON SOMEONE?
- No crush.
- Yes, blush!
- A new one every day.

8 EVER PASS A NOTE OR GIVE A PRESENT TO A CRUSH?
- Yes (sigh!)
- No (way!)

9 DO YOU LIKE SLEEPOVERS?
- Yes
- No

10 WHAT'S YOUR FAVORITE SLEEPOVER SNACK?
- Candy
- Chips
- Cookies or brownies
- Ice cream
- Pizza
- Popcorn
- None of the above

1

HOW OFTEN EACH WEEK DO YOU HANG OUT WITH ANY FRIENDS ANYWHERE?

Whether it's one day or every day, you've got plenty of company.

5, 6, 7 times a week? That's what 44% of kids say. And they sound very busy.

1 or 2 times a week? 34% think that's just right.

3 or 4 times a week? 22% of kids get together about half the time.

WEIRD-O-METER   1-2 = 2, 3-4 = 3, 5+ = 2

2 WHAT ABOUT THE NEIGHBORHOOD KIDS?

You want to know what's normal? Importing friends from other neighborhoods —THAT'S what's normal.

Spend a day with the neighbors? 32% spend 1 or 2 days.

Nobody good in the hood? 39% said zero.

Stay close to home close to 3 or 4 days each week? So do 20% of your friends.

Go loco for local friends most of the week? About 9% do.

WEIRD-O-METER   0 = 2, 1-2 = 2, 3-4 = 3, 5+ = 4

3 WHERE DO YOU AND YOUR PALS HANG OUT?

- 28% go wherever their friends are.
- 17% say pools and beaches make a splash.
- 12% prefer the mood— and food—at a friend's house.
- 12% hop to the shops at the mall.
- 9% hang with the homeboys and homegirls at home.
- 7% park it at the park.
- 5% actively prefer a sports facility.
- 3% order up a trip to a restaurant.
- and the other 7% take the party somewhere else.

WEIRD-O-METER   WHEREVER/POOL/FRIEND'S/MALL = 2, HOME/PARK/NONE OF THE ABOVE = 3, ANYTHING ELSE = 4

4

PICK ONE:
A FEW
BEST FRIENDS...
LOTS
...OR OF ACQUAINTANCES?

Rather keep it real? So do 7 out of 10 kids. They prefer quality to quantity.

Proud of a crowd? You've got a lot in common with a lot of kids—3 out of 10 want a bundle of buddies.

WEIRD-O-METER   CLOSE FRIENDS = 2, TONS OF BUDDIES= 3

5 WHAT'S THE TOP TOPIC WITH YOUR FRIENDS?

GOOD FRIENDS TALK. AND TALK. AND TALK. WHAT ABOUT?

Crushes crushed the other choices: 4 out of 10 say love conquers everything else.

Gossip, girls? Bad-mouth, boys? Behind-the-back chit-chat takes second place with a 3 out of 10.

40%

31%

8%

21%

Fashion and clothes aren't even close. Less than 1 in 10 says style's in style.

All the news that fits into lunchtime? Whatever's the latest is the greatest with 2 out of 10 kids.

WEIRD-O-METER CRUSH = 2, GOSSIP = 2, NEWS = 3, FASHION = 4

6

"BEEN DUMPED" BY A FRIEND?

EVER SAT DOWN AT LUNCH AND FOUND YOURSELF DESERTED?
You're in good (but bummed-out) company. 6 out of 10 kids have ended up in a friendship minus the friend.

If you've still got all the friends you started with, 4 out of 10 kids are in the same boat.

WEIRD-O-METER   YES = 2, NO = 3

7 GOT A CRUSH ON SOMEONE?

I have a huge crush, oh, yeah.
And so do 7 out of 10 of us.

Who? Me? No way! I'm 2
in 10, and that's fine.

Can you keep a secret? I'm the 1 in 10
who has a different crush all the time!

WEIRD-**O**-METER   YES = 1, NO = 3, DIFFERENT ALL THE TIME = 4

8 EVER PASS A NOTE

OR GIVE A PRESENT TO A CRUSH?

🌓 **ME? NO!** If you're one of the 2 out of 3 kids who kept their thoughts and their presents to themselves, you're normal. But don't expect it to last long. Once you get a major crush, *nothing* seems normal any more.

🌑 **OH, YES!** Giggle while you scribble? Feet lift when you sent that gift? You're one of the moon-eyed, goofy-smiled 1 out of 3.

WEIRD-**O**-METER   NO = 2, YES = 3

9 DO YOU LIKE SLEEP-OVERS?

What's the fastest way to find out if your friend snores? 5 out of 6 kids yell, "Sleepover!"

1 out of 6 says, "No sleepovers, thanks. I believe my friends when they say they're silent sleepers."

WEIRD-O-METER   YES = 1, NO = 4

10

WHAT'S YOUR FAVORITE SLEEPOVER SNACK?

PIZZA?
More than 1 in 4 likes a slice at a sleepover.

ICE CREAM?
About 1 in 6 kids gets the scoop.

COOKIES OR BROWNIES?
Nearly 1 in 7 mixes cookie sheets with bedsheets.

POPCORN?
About 1 in 7 goes to bed buttery.

CANDY?
1 out of 9 likes some sugar before sweet dreams.

CHIPS?
1 in 14 crunches a bunch.

NONE OF THE ABOVE
1 in 12 prefers something else entirely. What else is there?

WEIRD-O-METER   PIZZA/ICE CREAM = 2, ANYTHING ELSE = 3

WHERE ARE YOU ON THE WEIRD-O-METER?

TOTAL YOUR SCORE AND FIND OUT HOW YOU MEASURE AGAINST YOUR **FRIENDS.**

0-23

YOU'RE AS NORMAL AS SENDING YOUR FRIEND AN EMAIL.

You hang with the gang (but you're tight with your buds). You get the scoop from the group (but you can keep a secret). You're somewhere with somebody almost every day. Sure, some kids aren't your flavor, but you don't bug the ones who bug you. You take it easy.

20

10

0

50

24-29

YOU'RE AS NORMAL AS SEND-ING YOUR FRIEND A POSTCARD.

You don't stand out, but you don't exactly blend into the woodwork, either. You can go with the gang, or just as easily go it alone. Like the plans? Count you in. Not so interested? Check you later. You're unpredictable, and that suits you just fine.

30-40

YOU'RE AS NORMAL AS SENDING YOUR FRIEND A CLOWN-O-GRAM.

If the thought of being in a gang gives you gangrene, chances are you belong in this category. Like to make a splash, even when everyone else is swim-ming? Got an ever changing crush? Or no crush at all? You're not alone. (Unless you want to be!)

CAN YOU DO THIS?

IF YOU CAN DO THESE THINGS, YOU ARE DEFINITELY NOT NORMAL.

LICK

YOUR ELBOW? YOUR NOSE? YOUR CHIN?

MOVE EYES
IN OPPOSITE DIRECTIONS?

RAISE ONLY ONE EYEBROW?

MOVE ONE EYE BUT NOT THE OTHER?

TWITCH YOUR NOSE FROM SIDE TO SIDE?

TICKLE
YOURSELF AND GENUINELY LAUGH?

KEEP
FINGERS STRAIGHT
AND BEND ONLY THE JOINT
NEAR YOUR
FINGERTIPS.

STRETCH YOUR FINGERS AND MOVE ONLY
YOUR PINKY TO YOUR PALM?

PUT YOUR
ARM
BEHIND YOUR BACK
AND TOUCH AN EAR?

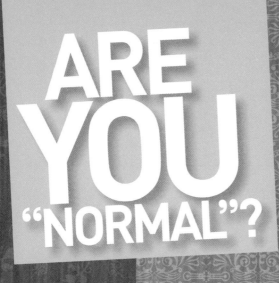

ARE YOU "NORMAL"?

FAMILY

FAMILY QUIZ

BE SURE TO KEEP TRACK OF YOUR ANSWERS!

1 HAVE YOU GOT A BROTHER OR SISTER?
- Yes
- No

2 HOW DO YOU SPEND TIME WITH YOUR FAMILY? (THE FIRST THING THAT COMES TO MIND!)
- Eat dinner
- Watch TV
- Talk
- Play sports
- Take a walk
- Do something else

3 HOW MANY OF YOUR PARENTS DO YOU LIVE WITH?
- Both parents
- Just Mom
- Dad only
- Someone else

4 DO YOU LIVE WITH A GRANDPARENT?
- I sure do.
- No, I don't.

OH BROTHER...

5 WERE YOU OR ONE OF YOUR PARENTS BORN OUTSIDE THE U.S.A?

Yes   No

6 SPEAK A LANGUAGE AT HOME THAT ISN'T ENGLISH?

Yes   No

7 WHAT DO YOU CALL THE MOM PERSON AT HOME?

- Mom or Mommy
- Mother
- We're on a first-name basis.
- Something else (hopefully, something nice)

8 WHAT DO YOU CALL THE DAD GUY AT HOME?

- Dad or Daddy
- Father
- We're first-name pals.
- Something different (he's different that way)

9 HOW OLD ARE YOU?

- 0-6
- 7-10
- 11-15
- 16-18
- 19+

10 WHO IN YOUR FAMILY GETS TO HEAR YOUR PROBLEMS FIRST?

- Mom
- Dad
- Sister
- Brother
- Grandparent
- Someone else (pets, cousins, etc.)

1 HAVE YOU GOT A BROTHER OR SISTER?

YES?

An astonishing 6 out of 7 kids have a sister (rhymes with "blister") or a brother (sort-of rhymes with "bother") or—*yikes!*—both!

NO?

If you're an only child, you're not alone. 1 out of 7 kids is an only child. (But who says "only" has to rhyme with "lonely"?)

 WEIRD-O-METER   YES = 1, NO = 4

2 HOW DO YOU SPEND TIME WITH YOUR FAMILY?

THE **FIRST** THING THAT COMES TO MIND!

GULP!
1 in 3 says, "We eat dinner."

34%

CLICK!
1 in 5 says, "We watch TV."

20%

14%

OMP!
ly 1
25 says,
e take
walk."

UM...
1 in 7 says, "We do something that is totally not on your list."

14%

14%

YAY!
1 in 7 says, "We like sports."

CHAT!
1 in 7 says, "We talk."

WEIRD-O-METER DINNER = 2, TV = 2, CHAT = 3, SPORTS = 3, SOMETHING ELSE = 3, WALK = 4

3 HOW MANY OF YOUR PARENTS
DO YOU LIVE WITH?

Almost 7 out of 10 kids **(67%)** live with **TWO PARENTS** at home.

Mom's the only parent in **25%** of the homes.

In **7%** of homes, Dad's holding down the fort.

WHOEVER'S IN CHARGE—MOM, DAD, OR SOMEONE ELSE—THE *REAL* QUESTION IS "WILL THEY LET YOU STAY UP LATE?"

WEIRD-O-METER BOTH = 1, JUST MOM = 3, DAD ONLY = 4, ANYTHING ELSE = 4

4

DO YOU LIVE WITH A GRANDPARENT?

NO

Not many kids enjoy the benefit of having a wise grandparent in the house. More than 9 out of 10 kids **(92%)** don't.

WEIRD-**O**-METER   NO = 1, YES = 4

5 WERE YOU OR ONE OF YOUR PARENTS BORN OUTSIDE the U.S.A.?

NO?

In 3 out of 4 of all American homes, the parents and kids were born in the U.S.A.

YES?

1 out of 4 homes has kids or a parent who came (by boat, airplane, car, etc.) from another country.

(If you came by spaceship, you are definitely an alien.)

IMMIGRATION
ARRIVED
3 1 JAN 2009
SYDNEY AIRPORT
515P
AUSTRALIA

WEIRD-O-METER   NO = 1, YES = 4

SPEAK A LANGUAGE AT HOME THAT **ISN'T** ENGLISH?

6

1 OUT OF 5 YES

OUI

SÍ

CAIN

DA

JA

NEH

4 OUT OF 5 NO

NOPE

NOT HAPPENING

NEGATIVE

NO WAY

WEIRD-**O**-METER   NO = 1, YES = 4

7 WHAT DO YOU CALL THE MOM PERSON AT HOME?

- **75 OUT OF 100 CALL THAT LADY "MOM" OR "MOMMY." ISN'T THAT WEIRD? IN ENGLAND, IT'S "MUM" OR "MUMMY."**

- Just 3 out of 100 kids go casual and use her first name.

- Another 3 out of 100 go formal and say "Mother."

- 19 out of 100 call her something else. Whether she answers or not depends on what name you use.

WEIRD-O-METER   MOM/MOMMY = 1,
SOMETHING ELSE = 3,
ANYTHING ELSE = 4

8 WHAT DO YOU CALL THE DAD GUY AT HOME?

- "DAD" AND "DADDY" PUT YOU IN THE SUPERNORMAL CATEGORY WITH 79 OUT OF 100 KIDS.

- 2 out of 100 call him something like "Father."

- 3 out of 100 call him "Mike" (if his name actually is Mike).

- 1 out of 6 calls him something different. But take our advice: "Yo! Hey you! Human ATM!" never works. Never, ever.

WEIRD-O-METER DAD/DADDY = 1, SOMETHING ELSE = 3, ANYTHING ELSE = 4

9 HOW OLD ARE YOU?

TRICK QUESTION. YOU'RE NORMAL NO MATTER WHAT AGE YOU ANSWER.

18 OR UNDER?
There are about four million other people in the U.S.A that are the same age as you. How many is four million? Imagine the entire population of Oregon (but with no adult in sight).

HAPPY BIRTHDAY!
About 11,000 people in the U.S.A. were born on the same day and year as you were. Now that's a lot of candles.

WEIRD-O-METER SCORE YOURSELF 2!

10

WHO IN YOUR FAMILY GETS TO

HEAR

YOUR PROBLEMS

FIRST?

- "MOM! HELP!" IS HEARD THE MOST. HALF OF ALL KIDS WANT THEIR MOM IN A JAM.

- "Dad!" Only 1 out of 6 kids turns to dad in a dilemma.

- Who says "S.O.S. Sis?" 1 out of every 12 kids. For brothers, it's the same 1 in 12. Together, sisters and brother tie with Dad at 1 out of 6.

- Grandparents = 1 in 20. Even though they've lived the longest and know a lot, for some reason it's not normal to ask the grandfolks for advice.

- Someone else? 1 in 9 asks a cousin, aunt, uncle, third cousin twice removed, goldfish, or whoever else could be considered family.

WEIRD-O-METER   MOM = 2, DAD = 2, SIS OR BRO = 3, SOMEONE ELSE = 3, GRANDPARENT = 4

WHERE ARE YOU ON THE WEIRD-O-METER?

ADD YOUR SCORES TO SEE IF YOU'RE THE MOST NORMAL PERSON IN YOUR **FAMILY.**

10

0

1-18

YOU'RE AS NORMAL AS CALLING YOUR MOM "MOM." They say the average American family has 2.3 kids. That's probably you! Maybe you get along with the other 1.3 kids, and maybe you sometimes squabble, but it's perfectly normal either way.

19-28 YOU'RE AS NORMAL AS CALLING YOUR MOM "SUSAN."

For you, the idea of "family" might be a bit more extended. Got a dog you dress up and call "Uncle Rover"? Sounds fun! You may live with mom and dad, but you may not. And who knows what language you sing "Happy Birthday" in? No matter how you slice it, it's still birthday cake.

20

30

40

29-40 YOU'RE AS NORMAL AS CALLING YOUR MOM "HEY, LADY!"

For you, the plain old family portrait just won't do. Because your family tree might look more like a forest, or maybe just a twig. In your house, weird is wonderful, and for that you can thank your parents . . . whoever they are.

ARE YOU "NORMAL"?

SPORTS QUIZ

BE SURE TO KEEP TRACK OF YOUR ANSWERS!

1 HOW IMPORTANT ARE SPORTS TO YOU?
- Really important
- Kind of important
- Sports? Huh?

2 HOW FAR IS THE MOST YOU'VE EVER RUN?
- 1 mile or less
- 2-4 miles
- 5-8 miles
- 9-12 miles
- Over 12 miles
- I'm not what you'd call a runner.

3 WANT TO BE ACTIVE IN MORE SPORTS?
- Yes
- No

4 FAVORITE SPORT TO PLAY? (NOT WATCH, PLAY!)
- Baseball
- Basketball
- Cheerleading
- Field hockey
- Football
- Gymnastics
- Hockey
- Ice skating
- Lacrosse
- Rollerblading
- Skateboarding
- Soccer
- Softball
- Volleyball
- Wrestling

5 LIKE YOUR SPORTS EXTREME?
- Yes, extreme!
- Yes, sports! No, extreme!
- No sports for me!

6 WATCH TV SPORTS OFTEN?
- Yes
- No

7 FAVORITE SPORT TO WATCH?
- Baseball
- Basketball
- Football
- Golf
- Ice hockey
- Soccer

8 DURING KID SPORTS, HAVE YOU EVER SEEN ANYONE'S PARENTS ... YELL TOO LOUDLY?
- Yes
- No

9 ... ARGUE WITH THE COACHES?
- Yes
- No

1 HOW IMPORTANT ARE SPORTS TO YOU?

🔵 **BREATHE BASKETBALL?** Have faith in football? Hail hockey? Go team! If sports are really important to you, you're really normal. And so are more than a third of your classmates.

🔵 **LIKE A GOOD GAME?** Can name some players? Maybe you own something with your team's name on it? If sports are sometimes kind of important, you're just as normal as the sports nuts! More than a third feel the same way.

🔵 **NEED TO HAVE A GRAND SLAM EXPLAINED?** Can't tell your field goals from your extra points? If sports is just noise while you're changing the channels, you're pretty normal, too. A quarter of the kids just can't be bothered.

WEIRD-O-METER VERY = 2, KIND OF = 2, NOT AT ALL = 3

2 HOW FAR IS THE MOST YOU'VE EVER RUN?

1 MILE OR LESS?
You've pulled into the lead. A third of the kids keep it local.

2-4 MILES?
You're on the road to normal. 1 in 5 kids is on your training schedule.

5-8 MILES?
You're still in the running for a strong finish. 1 in 12 has logged that kind of mileage.

9-12 MILES?
Way to go. And go. At 1 in 20 you're not normal, but you get around.

OVER 12 MILES?
Keep going forth: a fourth of all kids say they've hit the road hard. FYI, 13 miles is a half-marathon. And a whole achievement.

RUNNING'S NOT YOUR THING?
Don't sweat it. 1 in 8 says they would rather be late than run out of breath.

WEIRD-O-METER 1 OR LESS = 2, 2-4 = 2, 5-8 = 3, 9-12 = 4, 12+ = 2, NOT A RUNNER = 3

3

WANT TO BE
ACTIVE
IN MORE
SPORTS?

4 OUT OF 10 SAID **YES! COACH!** PUT ME IN THE BIG GAME!

6 out of 10 said **NO! SERIOUSLY!** I'm game to keep things the way they are!

WEIRD-**O**-METER   NO = 2, YES =3

4

FAVORITE SPORT TO PLAY? (NOT WATCH, PLAY!)

HOW DO YOU BEST GET YOUR KICKS?

21% SOCCER

16% BASKETBALL

10% BASEBALL

10% CHEERLEADING

8% FOOTBALL

7% GYMNASTICS

7% VOLLEYBALL

4% SOFTBALL

4% ICE SKATING

3% SKATEBOARDING

3% ROLLERBLADING

2% WRESTLING

2% HOCKEY

2% LACROSSE

1% FIELD HOCKEY

WEIRD-O-METER SOCCER, BASKETBALL, BASEBALL, CHEERLEADING, FOOTBALL, GYMNASTICS, VOLLEYBALL = 2, SOFTBALL, ICE SKATING = 3, EVERYTHING ELSE = 4

5 LIKE YOUR SPORTS

EXTR

○ **YES, I'M EXTREME-LY INTO EXTREME SPORTS! (55%)**

◑ I'm a good sport, but only the regular ones. (35%)

◔ The only thing I surf is channels. (10%)

EME?

6 WATCH TV SPORTS OFTEN?

WHO DO YOU THINK WATCHES MORE TV SPORTS, **GIRLS OR BOYS?** THE ANSWERS AREN'T AS FAR APART AS YOU MIGHT GUESS.

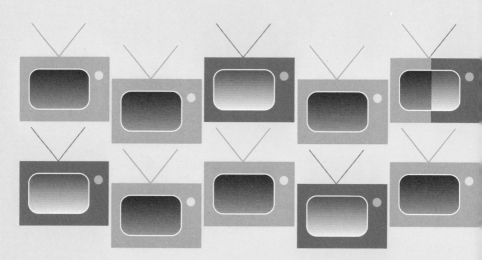

WHO SAID **YES,** THEY REGULARLY GET THEIR SPORTS FROM THE BEST SEATS IN THE HOUSE?

More than 6 in 10 boys

Almost 4 in 10 girls

WEIRD-O-METER GIRLS—NO = 2, YES = 3
BOYS—YES = 2, NO = 3

FAVORITE SPORT TO WATCH?

7

We have a winner! The hoop and the goalposts shoot past home plate and the end zone!

#1
RANKING
BASKETBALL (27%)

#2
RANKING
SOCCER
(24%)

#3
RANKING
BASEBALL
(16%)

#4
RANKING
FOOTBALL
(15%)

#5
RANKING
ICE HOCKEY
(9%)

#6
RANKING
GOLF
(6%)

WEIRD-O-METER BASKETBALL = 2, SOCCER = 2, BASEBALL = 3
FOOTBALL = 3, ICE HOCKEY = 3, GOLF = 4

8 DURING KID SPORTS, HAVE YOU EVER SEEN ANYONE'S PARENTS...

...YELL TOO LOUDLY?

7 OUT OF 10 KIDS SCREAMED **YES!**

3 out of 10 whispered **NO.**

WEIRD-O-METER YES = 2, NO = 3

9 ...ARGUE WITH COACHES?

3 OUT OF 10 KIDS SAID **YES!**

7 out of 10 kids said **NO,** and thank goodness!

WEIRD-O-METER NO = 2, YES = 3

WHERE ARE YOU ON THE WEIRD-O-METER?

COMBINE YOUR SCORES AND DISCOVER IF YOU'RE A TEAM PLAYER OR A SOLO SPORTSMAN.

0-22

YOU'RE AS NORMAL AS CALLING AMERICAN FOOTBALL "FOOTBALL."

With sports, normal runs straight down the center. You like to play sometimes, and if you aren't on a team right now, you probably were a player not long ago. It's perfectly normal to have team logos on your clothes, but you don't wear them head to toe. Yet.

9

0

23-27

YOU'RE AS NORMAL AS CALLING SOCCER "FOOTBALL."

You scored here? Then step up the sports loving (or hating) a notch more. You might have a regular team. You might be a major-league avoider. Either way, you're probably pretty good at it. One thing's for sure, you don't take it to the extreme.

28-36

YOU'RE AS NORMAL AS CALLING PING-PONG "FOOTBALL."

Sportswise, you're on the far end of normal. That means you're either a massive jock or a massive couch-jockey. And whichever way you play it, professional sports teams will leave you one of two ways: uniformed or uninformed. That means during the Super Bowl, people will find you screaming for your team in face paint . . . or they'll find you sound asleep in the bowl of pretzels.

18

27

36

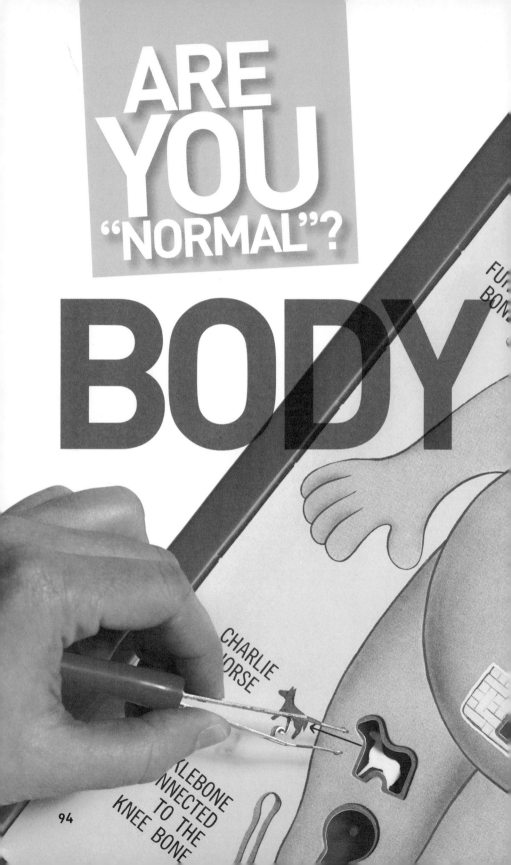

ARE YOU "NORMAL"?

BODY

FU...
BON...

CHARLIE
HORSE

...KLEBONE
...NNECTED
TO THE
KNEE BONE

94

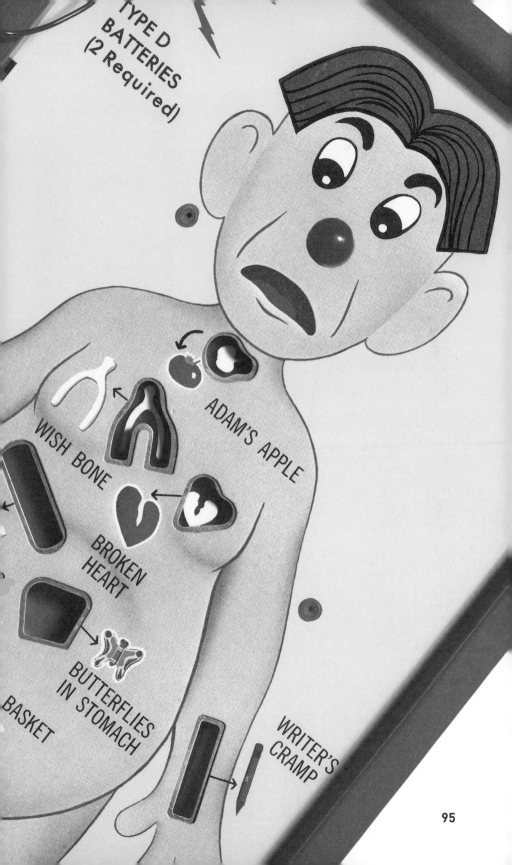

BODY QUIZ

BE SURE TO KEEP TRACK OF YOUR ANSWERS!

1 DO YOU BITE YOUR FINGERNAILS?
- Yes
- No

2 DO YOU BITE YOUR TOENAILS?
- Yes
- No

3 HOW MANY HOURS DO YOU SLEEP?
- 8+ hours
- 6-7 hours
- 5 hours or less

4 DO YOU PICK YOUR SCABS?
- Yes
- No

5 DO YOU WEAR BRACES?
- Yes (I do)
- Yes (I did)
- Not yet
- No

6 DO YOU FLOSS?
- Once a day
- Once a week
- Hardly ever

7 WHAT COLOR HAIR DO YOU HAVE?
- Blond
- Brunette
- Red
- Black
- Bald

8 EVER FAKED SICK TO MISS SCHOOL?
- Yes
- No

9 ARE YOU:
- Right handed
- Left handed
- Both

1 DO YOU **BITE** YOUR FINGERNAILS?

YOU'RE NORMAL EITHER WAY.

YUM, YES.
Half the kids say it's a handy snack at test time. Perhaps it's a good source of calcium?

THE OTHER HALF SAYS NO THANKS.
Even do-it-yourself manicures require a pair of clippers.

WEIRD-**O**-METER SCORE YOURSELF 2!

2 DO YOU BITE YOUR TOENAILS?

ABSOLUTELY NOT.
9 out of 10 say no, as in
"Could I even do that?"

**ABSOLUTELY ... WELL ...
MAYBE.**
1 in 10 kids has a spine as
flexible as their diet plan.

WEIRD-O-METER   NO = 1, YES = 4

3 HOW MANY HOURS DO YOU SLEEP?

DO YOU SNORE FOR 8 OR MORE?
Half of all kids say they're well rested.

GET 40 WINKS FOR 6 TO 7 HOURS?
1 in 3 says it's not beauty sleep, but it's pretty good.

STAY AWAKE FOR 19 HOURS OR MORE?
1 in 5 gets 5 hours or less every 24 hours,
and that's . . .

. . . ZZZZZZZZ

WEIRD-**O**-METER   8+ = 2, 6-7 = 2, 5 OR LESS = 3

4 DO YOU PICK YOUR SCABS?

YES. 43% of kids think scabs are nature's way of saying, "Here's something new to play with."

NO. 57% say they never do it, or they've never tried.

WEIRD-**O**-METER   NO = 2, YES = 3

5 DO YOU WEAR BRACES?

NO! About 40% of kids gave us the straight news about their straight teeth.

YES! About 20% of kids set off the metal detector when they smile.

IT'S COMING! 34% of all kids say they've got a future date (or 80) with the orthodontist.

GLEAM! Been there, done that. 6% ex-metal mouths will blind you with their dazzling dental work. Pass the gum!

WEIRD-O-METER NO = 2, NOT YET = 2, YES (I DO) = 3, YES (I DID) = 4

6 DO YOU FLOSS?

EVERY DAY? You're 1 in 3 for normal, and #1 for good-looking, healthy teeth. You shine!

EVERY WEEK? Just 1 in 8 kids slides a string between the pearly whites each week. Not so bad, but not so good either.

HARDLY EVER? Over half of all kids can't be bothered. That's okay, the world needs jack-o'-lanterns. Bad for you, good for the dentist.

WEIRD-O-METER HARDLY EVER = 2, ONCE A DAY = 2, ONCE A WEEK = 4

7 HAIR YE! HAIR YE!

WHAT HAIR HAVE YE?

Brown and beautiful? Over a half have it.

57%

Black and brilliant? It even shines at night.

4%

12%

27%

Blond and bright? A quarter say yay.

Red and remarkable? 1 in 20 has red aplenty.

BALD AS A BOWLING BALL? NOT YET! (0%)

WEIRD-O-METER BROWN = 2, BLOND = 2, RED = 3, BLACK = 4, BALD = 4

8 EVER FAKED SICK TO MISS SCHOOL?

YES?

Can you come up with a cough? Fake a fever? Play plague? 1 in 4 kids has used acting skills to act pathetic on a school day. It's okay, you're not alone—you're not even contagious.

NO?

What? Violate the sacred trust between a scholar and an institution by defrauding my very own family? Me??? Never! Or, not yet. Either way, 3 out of 4 kids *say* they've been good.

WEIRD-O-METER   NO = 1, YES = 3

9 LEFT HANDED OR...

About 15 out of 100 people are left handed. And you know what that means . . .

RIGHT HANDED = 1, LEFT HANDED = 4, AMBIDEXTROUS = 4

...RIGHT HANDED?

Most of us (85 out of 100) write with our right. Being right handed is so normal, they named it "right." Right?

Don't consider yourself to be left or right handed? Don't worry. You're not alone. Some people are ambidextrous (say that 10 times fast), meaning they can write with their left or right hand. Scientists aren't sure how many are like this, but it's way cool and definitely not normal!

WHERE ARE YOU ON THE WEIRD-O-METER?

TOTAL THE NUMBERS AND COMPARE WITH EVERYBODY ABOUT YOUR **BODY.**

0-20

YOU'RE AS NORMAL AS BRUSHING YOUR TEETH.

You ended up here? It's all in the genes, baby! Straight teeth (from all that nail biting), wide awake (from all that sleep), probably brown hair (from all those ancestors), and luckiest of all, you're most likely right handed. If you ask any lefty, almost everything is set up for righties because almost everyone is right handed.

0

9

26-36

YOU'RE AS NORMAL AS PAINTING YOUR TEETH.

As you know, you've got a look and style that's all your own. You stand out from the crowd. Be proud: you can probably be picked out of a yearbook much faster than anyone "normal." That makes you the person people will remember best.

21-25

YOU'RE AS NORMAL AS FLOSSING YOUR TEETH.

Okay, you're not like the majority, but is that bad? Maybe it's flaming red hair, or some unique, left-handed handwriting that gives you a personal flair. Maybe you keep all your scabs exactly where they belong. Or you floss so much that you forget to pull the strings out of your mouth. That will certainly get you noticed!

18   27   36

CAN YOU DO THIS?

IF YOU CAN DO THESE THINGS, YOU ARE DEFINITELY NOT NORMAL.

PUT YOUR FOOT BEHIND YOUR HEAD?

PUT ALL YOUR TOES IN YOUR MOUTH?
(WHY WOULD YOU?)

PUT YOUR WHOLE FIST IN YOUR MOUTH?
THIS IS EASIER FOR GIRLS.

MOVE YOUR ARMS
IN CIRCLES LIKE
WINDMILLS
THEN
SWITCH
THE DIRECTION OF ONE ARM WITHOUT SLOWING THE OTHER ARM DOWN.

IF YOU CAN MOVE THEM IN
OPPOSITE CIRCLES
AT THE SAME TIME, YOU'RE REALLY
NOT NORMAL!

ARE YOU "NORMAL"?

TECH QUIZ

BE SURE TO KEEP
TRACK OF YOUR
ANSWERS!

1 NAME YOUR FAVORITE HANDHELD GADGET.
- Cell phone
- Camera
- Music player
- Video game

2 PLAY VIDEO GAMES?
- All the time
- Sometimes
- Nope, don't like them
- Nope, not allowed

3 WHAT'S THE TOP THING YOU DO ONLINE?
- Watch (videos)
- Play (games)
- Do (homework)
- Hang (with friends)
- Or (something else)

4 HAVE YOU READ A DIGITAL E-BOOK YET?
- Yes, I have.
- Not yet, but I'd like to.
- No, I'll take paper, please.

5 HOW MANY TEXTS DO YOU SEND A DAY?

- None
- Between 1 and 24
- More than 24

6 COULD YOU SHUT OFF YOUR COMPUTER AND TV FOR A WHOLE WEEK? (THAT'S SEVEN DAYS!)

- Yes
- Maybe yes
- No
- Maybe no

7 HAVE A COMPUTER AT HOME?

- Yes
- No, not yet

8 HOW MANY SONGS ARE YOUR MP3 PLAYER?

- I don't have an MP3 player.
- Over 1,000 songs
- Fewer than 50 songs
- 51-100 songs
- 101-500 songs
- 501-1,000 songs

1 NAME YOUR FAVORITE HANDHELD GADGET

RING! Cell phones push more kids' buttons, with over 4 out of 10 kids answering that way.

CLICK! Cameras made most of the kids shudder. Just 1 in 10 would pocket the point-and-click.

SING! 3 in 10 sang the praises of their mighty mini music players.

BANG! If you think video games are the top scorers, you'd better reboot. Only 2 in 10 put them first.

WEIRD-O-METER CELL PHONE = 2, MUSIC PLAYER = 2, VIDEO GAME = 3, CAMERA = 4

2 PLAY
VIDEO GAMES?

YES. 43% of kids say, "I play so much I could do push ups with my thumbs. Level 252 anyone?"

SOMETIMES. Another 39% say, "I win some, I lose some, I go outside some."

NO. 12% of kids say, "No, I just don't like 'em."

WORSE THAN NO. 6% of kids say, "No, I'm not allowed!"

WEIRD-**O**-METER ALL THE TIME = 2, SOMETIMES = 2, NOPE, DON'T LIKE 'EM = 3, NOPE, NOT ALLOWED = 3

3 WHAT'S THE TOP THING YOU DO ONLINE?

You'd think the Internet was invented just so kids could play. More than half said gaming was what Wi-Fi was for.

➤ Keeping up with friends, chatting, posting, and otherwise hanging out online is number one with 1 out of 8 kids.

➤ Videos, viral or not, are the next big thing. 1 in 10 kids thinks www means wonderful, watchable web.

➤ 1 in 20 kids uses the Internet mostly to make their homework load go down and their grades go up.

➤ And if you do something else online, you're not alone. 1 in 6 kids reports none of the above. Whatever it is, hope it's fun!

WEIRD-O-METER   PLAY GAMES = 2, WATCH VIDEOS = 3, HANG WITH FRIENDS = 3, SOMETHING ELSE = 3, HOMEWORK = 4

4

HAVE YOU READ A DIGITAL E-BOOK YET?

NOT YET
57% of kids say they haven't read an e-book yet, but they get wired just thinking about it.

YOU BET
So far, 25% of kids have already read an e-book.

E-BOOK? EGADS!
And 18% of kids prefer their books bound, their paper printed, and their info inked.

1
2
3
4
5
6
7
8
9
0

MEN

HOW MANY TEXTS
DO YOU SEND A DAY?

IF YOUR AVERAGES ARE NEAR THESE, YOU'RE PRETTY NORMAL.

BOYS 9-10: 3/DAY
BOYS 11-13: 11/DAY

GIRLS 9-10: 4/DAY
GIRLS 11-13: 24/DAY

IF THE NUMBERS SEEM LOW, THAT'S BECAUSE FOR EVERY KID WHO SENDS 200 A DAY, LOTS OF KIDS DON'T SEND ANY, OR EVEN HAVE A PHONE.

WEIRD-O-METER   0-24 = 2, 24+ = 3

6

COULD YOU SHUT OFF YOUR COMPUTER FOR A WHOLE WEEK?
(THAT'S SEVEN DAYS!)

YES
Well, well, well . . . will-power is normal. Almost half the kids could do time without screen time.

NO
You're in good company. 1 in 3 kids admits they can't break connection.

MAYBE
Maybe yes? Or maybe no? We can't tell. Either way, 1 out of 5 can't make up their mind about shutting down for a week.

WEIRD-O-METER   YES = 2, NO = 2, MAYBE = 3

7 DO YOU HAVE A COMPUTER AT HOME?

○ Having a computer in your home is the new normal. Very, very normal. More than 8 in 10 kids have access to one at home.

◔ 2 in 10 kids don't have a computer in their homes. Yet.

These numbers keep on changing. Not so long ago, having phones, TVs, and indoor toilets wasn't normal either.

WEIRD-O-METER YES = 1, NO = 4

HOW MANY SONGS ARE ON YOUR MP3 PLAYER?

➤ 14% of kids have over 1,000 songs.

➤ 10% of kids have fewer than 50 songs.

➤ 8% of kids have 51-100 songs.

➤ 8% of kids have 101-500 songs.

➤ And to prove it's either all or nothing, only 5% have between 501-1,000 songs.

➤ If you don't have an MP3 player, that's pretty normal. 51% of kids don't either.

WEIRD-O-METER

1,000+ = 2, LESS THAN 50 = 2,
51-100 = 3, 101-500 = 3, 501-1,000 = 4,
NO MP3 PLAYER = 2

WHERE ARE YOU ON THE WEIRD-O-METER?

TALLY YOUR ANSWERS TO SEE IF YOU'RE WEIRD ABOUT **TECH.**

1-22

YOU'RE AS NORMAL AS WATCHING TV.
When it comes to electronics, you can tech it or leave it. Games, machines, web sites, apps and programs may come and go, but that won't stop you from sticking to your favorites. You know what you like, even if it's—gasp!—a book. Online, offline—everything lines up fine for you.

0   9

LOADING...

23-27

YOU'RE AS NORMAL AS WATCHING TV ON A PHONE.

Do you watch a movie, surf the Web, send a text, and write your homework in different windows at the same time? Do you text friends who are in the same room? Then you're on your way to being a total techie. Someday, but not yet.

27   36

28-36

YOU'RE AS NORMAL AS WATCHING TV WIRED TO YOUR BRAIN.

Chances are, technology really pushes your buttons. How many gadgets do you have that can send a message / take a picture/play music/do your homework/play dodgeball for you? If you answered "a lot" then you need the latest and greatest. Got a gadget to wash your clothes? Just Mom or Dad? You see? You still do some things the old-fashioned way.

ARE YOU "NORMAL"?

FOOD

FOOD QUIZ

BE SURE TO KEEP TRACK OF YOUR ANSWERS!

1 WHERE DO YOU BITE THE **CHOCOLATE BUNNY** FIRST?
- The ears
- The tail
- The feet
- Who cares? It's chocolate!

2 IF FOOD THAT'S NEW MAKES YOU SAY P.U., WELL, WHAT DO YOU DO?
- Dive right in
- Take a tiny taste
- Hide it
- Dump it on Rover

3 PIZZA! PIZZA! HOW DO YOU LIKE YOUR SLICE?
- Hot and cheesy
- Popping with pepperoni
- With the works
- Something else

4 DO YOU CUT UP OR WIND YOUR SPAGHETTI?
- Cut it up
- Wind it up
- Don't eat it either way

5 HOW'S THAT PEANUT BUTTER? SMOOTH OR CHUNKY?
- Smooth
- Chunky
- No thanks!

6 IT'S NOT PEANUT BUTTER WITHOUT...
- Bananas
- Chocolate
- Fluff
- Jelly

7 WHAT'S YOUR FAVORITE JUICE?
- Apple
- Grapefruit
- Orange
- Tomato
- No! No! No juice!

8 DO YOU USUALLY EAT GOOD-FOR-YOU FOOD?
- Always
- Sometimes
- When I'm being watched
- No (burp!)

9 WHAT'S YOUR FAVORITE THANKSGIVING LEFTOVER?
- Cranberries
- Gravy
- Pie
- Rolls
- Stuffing
- Turkey
- Veggies

10 WHICH ICE CREAM FLAVOR MAKES YOU MELT?
- Strawberry
- Butter pecan
- Chocolate chip
- Praline pecan
- Vanilla
- Rocky road
- Cherry
- Coffee
- Chocolate
- Cookies and cream
- Vanilla fudge ripple
- Chocolate almond
- Chocolate marshmallow
- French vanilla
- Neopolitan
- Something else

1 WHERE DO YOU BITE THE CHOCOLATE BUNNY FIRST?

Hear this: Over half eat the ears first.

Fluffy fact: 1 in 25 tastes the tail first.

Who cares? 1 out of 3 just grabs, bites, and chews.

Hop to it: 1 in 25 feasts on the feet first.

WEIRD-O-METER   EARS = 2, ANYWHERE = 2, TAIL = 4, FEET = 4

2 IF FOOD THAT'S NEW MAKES YOU SAY P.U., WELL WHAT DO YOU DO?

- A third of the kids would prefer to pass it off to a dog, cat, hamster, or little sister.

- Almost a third will happily dive right in.

- A quarter of the kids will try a little bite, but no promises!

- And 1 in 6 kids will play magician, take a napkin, and make the offending food disappear.

WEIRD-O-METER   FEED IT = 2, TASTE IT = 2, TRY IT = 3, HIDE IT = 3

3 PIZZA! PIZZA!

HOW DO YOU LIKE YOUR SLICE?

4 in 10 say hot and cheesy is really pleasing!

Another 4 in 10 say pepperoni gives them pep!

Something else? That's just not normal! Fewer than 1 in 10 eat it your way.

With the works works for fewer than 1 in 10 kids.

WEIRD-O-METER CHEESE = 2, PEPPERONI = 2, THE WORKS = 4, SOMETHING ELSE = 4

4

DO YOU CUT UP OR WIND YOUR SPAGHETTI?

In the great debate between winding and cutting, the winders win.

82% of kids give their spaghetti a spin.

15% of kids give it the knife.

And a few—3%—say they don't eat the stuff at all. Does that include macaroni?

WEIRD-**O**-METER   WIND IT = 1, CUT IT = 4, DON'T EAT IT = 4

5

HOW'S THAT PEANUT BUTTER?
SMOOTH
OR CHUNKY?

➤ Just over half of you spread the smooth.

➤ Just over a quarter of the kids cheer for chunky.

➤ The rest of the kids won't go near the stuff. That's 1 in 5 for tuna fish.

6

IT'S NOT PEANUT BUTTER WITHOUT...

42% THINK JELLY IS YOUR JAM.

27% CHOCK ONE UP FOR CHOCOLATE.

16% GO APE FOR BANANAS.

15% KNOW FLUFF IS THE STUFF.

WEIRD-O-METER JELLY = 2, CHOCOLATE = 2, BANANAS = 3, MARSHMALLOW FLUFF = 3

⁷APPLE! ORANGE! TOMATO! OH MY!

WHAT'S YOUR FAVORITE JUICE?

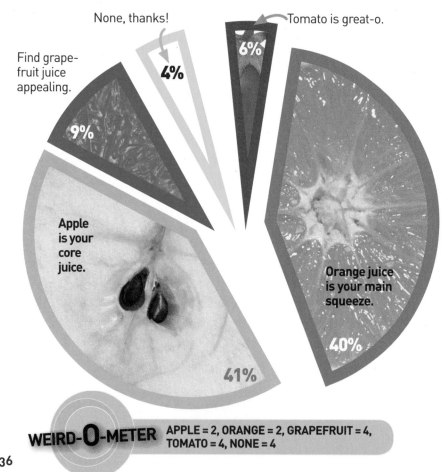

None, thanks!

Tomato is great-o.

Find grape-fruit juice appealing.

9%

4%

6%

Apple is your core juice.

Orange juice is your main squeeze.

41%

40%

WEIRD-**O**-METER APPLE = 2, ORANGE = 2, GRAPEFRUIT = 4, TOMATO = 4, NONE = 4

8

DO YOU USUALLY EAT

GOOD-FOR-YOU FOOD?

- Just over half say, "Smart sometimes, but mmm that junk food . . ."
- 1 in 4 says, "Me eat healthy. Me strong!"
- About 1 in 6 says, "I eat like PacMan, but not nearly as well."
- Almost 1 in 20 says, "Only when grownups are watching."

WEIRD-O-METER SOMETIMES = 2, NOT REALLY = 2, ALWAYS = 3, ONLY WHEN GROWNUPS ARE WATCHING = 4

9 WHAT'S YOUR FAVORITE THANKSGIVING LEFTOVER?

It's a leftover tie between turkey and pie! (45%)

Craving carbs? 4% of you feast on rolls.

3% stuff stuffing.

One thing's for sure, it's definitely not normal to crave cranberries (1%) . . .

. . . gobble gravy (1%) . . .

. . . or beg for veggies (1%).

WEIRD-O-METER TURKEY OR PIE = 2, ALL OTHER ANSWERS = 4

10 WHICH ICE CREAM FLAVOR MAKES YOU MELT?

Flavor	%
VANILLA	**29.0%**
CHOCOLATE	8.9%
BUTTER PECAN	5.3%
STRAWBERRY	5.3%
NEAPOLITAN	4.2%
CHOCOLATE CHIP	3.9%
FRENCH VANILLA	3.8%
COOKIES & CREAM	3.6%
VANILLA FUDGE RIPPLE	2.6%
PRALINE PECAN	1.7%
CHERRY	1.6%
CHOCOLATE ALMOND	1.6%
COFFEE	1.6%
ROCKY ROAD	1.5%
CHOCOLATE MARSHMALLOW	1.3%
SOMETHING ELSE	24.1%

WEIRD-O-METER VANILLA, CHOCOLATE, AND SOMETHING ELSE = 2, BUTTER PECAN, STRAWBERRY, NEOPOLITAN, CHOCOLATE CHIP, FRENCH VANILLA, AND COOKIES AND CREAM = 3, ALL OTHER ANSWERS = 4

WHERE ARE YOU ON THE WEIRD-O-METER?

ADD UP THE RESULTS TO SEE HOW NORMAL YOU ARE ABOUT **FOOD.**

0-21

YOU'RE AS NORMAL AS KETCHUP ON A HOT DOG.

There are no surprises when it comes to you and food. Which means you're always reliable. Hamburgers? Spaghetti? Mac and cheese? Yes, please. Escargot? I don't think so . . . that's fancy talk for snails. One thing's for sure, you make a trip to the grocery store a piece of cake. (Mmm . . . cake!)

2-27

YOU'RE AS NORMAL AS KETCHUP ON EGGS.

Sure you like a chicken nugget as much as the next kid, but you'll also venture outside your comfort zone. Forget tomato sauce on your pizza, maybe you'll try the pesto instead. No mozzarella? That's okay, how about cheese from a goat? A buffalo? Don't push it. More often than not, when it comes to food you're easy to please.

28-36

YOU'RE AS NORMAL AS KETCHUP ON A WATERMELON.

You just don't go by the book —the cookbook, that is. Why have chicken for lunch when pigeons are so easy to find? How's that sardine and peanut butter sandwich? Does it need more mustard? Let's face it: if it's edible, it's credible. Whether fancy French cuisine or your little brother's pickle-and-pretzel cold cereal, you'll happily bring your own shovel-size spoon.

18

27

36

CAN YOU DO THIS?

IF YOU CAN DO THESE THINGS, YOU ARE DEFINITELY NOT NORMAL.

SIT ON THE FLOOR

LIFT AND STRETCH OUT YOUR RIGHT LEG. MOVE YOUR LEG IN CLOCKWISE CIRCLE. NOW MOVE YOUR RIGHT ARM IN A COUNTERCLOCKWISE CIRCLE.

STAND

SIDEWAYS WITH YOUR ENTIRE SIDE

(ARMS
AND LEGS)

AGAINST A WALL. NOW
LIFT YOUR OTHER

FOOT (WITHOUT LOSING

CONTACT WITH THE WALL).

PUT YOUR HAND DOWN ON A TABLE AND

SPREAD OUT
YOUR FINGERS.

TUCK YOUR MIDDLE FINGER
UNDER SO THE NAIL TOUCHES
YOUR PALM. NOW LIFT YOUR

RING FINGER.

ARE YOU "NORMAL"?

BET-

144

ME QUIZ

BE SURE TO KEEP TRACK OF YOUR ANSWERS!

1 DO YOU LIKE YOUR NAME?
- I love it all.
- I don't like my first name.
- I can't stand my last name.
- I would change my whole name if I could.

2 DO YOU COOK?
- Always
- Sometimes
- Never

CRUNCH!

3 WHICH SUPERPOWER WOULD MAKE YOUR CAPE FLUTTER?
- Flying
- Super speed
- Super strength
- Super stretching
- Invisibility

4 WHAT'S THE MEANEST THING YOU COULD DO?
- Talk behind someone's back
- Call people names, or make fun of them
- Act all snobby
- Lie or brag
- Hit or bully somebody

5 WHO ON THIS LIST DO YOU ADMIRE MOST?

- Teachers
- Scientists
- Politicians
- Actors
- Athletes

6 PICK A GIFT, ANY GIFT. IT'S FOR YOU!

- A new bike
- A TV
- A computer or iPod
- A video game or console
- Something else

7 SCHOOL NIGHT! WHAT TIME DOES YOUR BEDTIME SENTENCE BEGIN?

- 7-8 p.m.
- 8-9 p.m.
- 9-10 p.m.
- 10-11 p.m.
- 11 p.m.-12 a.m.
- 12 a.m. or later

8 HOW TRENDY ARE YOU?

- Is it new? I want it.
- I do a mix of new and old.
- I'm strictly classic.

147

1

DO YOU LIKE YOUR NAME?

HERE'S HOW MANY KIDS WOULD CHANGE THEIR LABEL, IF THEY WERE ABLE.

The majority of kids are happy to say, "Both of my names have got game." **(57%)**

"My whole name is totally lame." **(19%)**

"Only my last name is to blame." **(18%)**

"Just my first name is a shame." **(6%)**

WEIRD-O-METER LOVE IT = 1, LAST NAME = 3, TOTALLY LAME = 3, FIRST NAME = 4

2 DO YOU COOK?

→ 42% All the time! I'm a chef!
→ 46% Sometimes! If it's easy.
→ 12% Never. Ever.

WEIRD-O-METER ALWAYS = 2, SOMETIMES = 2, NEVER = 4

3

WHICH SUPERPOWER WOULD MAKE YOUR CAPE FLUTTER?

It's not hard to see why invisibility is the most normal—8 out of 20 kids want to go where they're not supposed to.

5 out of 20 kids would zip for super speed.

Ever want to go up, up, and away? 4 out of 20 kids want to fly.

Super strength isn't such a strong choice. It's only a smash with 2 in 20 kids.

And stretching powers are a real stretch from normal. Only 1 kid in every 20 can get their arms around *that* superpower.

POW!!

CRUNCH!

BAM!!

WEIRD-O-METER INVISIBILITY AND SUPER SPEED = 2, FLYING = 3, SUPER STRENGTH AND SUPER STRETCH = 4

4

WHAT'S THE
MEANEST
THING YOU COULD DO?

KIDS AGREE: *ALL* OF THESE BAD THINGS ARE BAD NEWS, AND ARE PRETTY MUCH TIED.

➤ Hitting and bullying are definitely the worst. (28%) But all the rest aren't far behind.

➤ So DON'T talk behind someone's back. (21%)

➤ Please DON'T act all snobby. (19%)

➤ Certainly DON'T lie or brag. (18%)

➤ DON'T make fun of people or call them names. (14%)

WEIRD-O-METER TALKING BEHIND BACK AND HITTING/BULLYING = 2, ANYTHING ELSE = 3

5 WHO ON THIS LIST DO YOU ADMIRE MOST?

ATHLETES? Score with 36%!

TEACHERS? 23% give them an "A."

ACTORS? 23% roll out the red carpet.

SCIENTISTS? Where's the chemistry? Only 15% here.

And only 6% voted for **POLITICIANS.**

WEIRD-O-METER ATHLETES, TEACHERS, AND ACTORS = 2, SCIENTISTS = 3, POLITICIANS = 4

6

PICK A GIFT, ANY GIFT. IT'S FOR YOU!

If you want a computer or iPod, that's normal. (34%)

Not so many kids want a game console or video game. (16%)

There's nothing new about a new bike—not a lot of kids needed one. (9%)

And turn off the TV—hardly anyone wanted that. (5%)

Actually, the winner was none of the above—with 36% wanting something else. Maybe a pet piranha, a trip to Mount Everest, or a helicopter? Something boring like that.

WEIRD-O-METER IPOD AND NONE OF THE ABOVE = 2, VIDEO GAME = 3, ANYTHING ELSE = 4

153

7 SCHOOL NIGHT!
WHAT TIME DOES YOUR BEDTIME SENTENCE BEGIN?

Hit the hay between 10 and 11? With 13%, that's later than most.

Up, up, up until 11 or 12? With only 5%, there's nothing normal about that.

15% are burning the midnight oil. No wonder so many of you are napping in class!

Lights out between 9 and 10? 30% of kids are counting sheep by then.

Nighty-night between 8 and 9? With 25%, you're not alone!

10% hit the hay between 7 and 8. Not so normal (unless you're still little).

WEIRD-O-METER 7-8 = 3, 8-9 = 2, 9-10 = 2, 10-11 = 3, 11-12 = 4, 12+ = 3

8 HOW TRENDY ARE YOU?

NEW? OLD? A MASH-UP OF BOTH? WHATEVER... YOU'RE NORMAL!

- Is only new true to you? 8 out of 20 kids agree.
- Gotta have the famous original traditional classic style? That's 7 out of 20.
- And if a slick mix does the trick, it's about 5 out of 20.

WEIRD-O-METER ALL NEW = 2, CLASSIC = 2, MIX OF NEW AND OLD = 3

WHERE ARE YOU ON THE WEIRD-O-METER?

COMBINE YOUR RESULTS AND SEE IF THERE'S ANYONE WEIRDER THAN ME.

YOU'RE AS NORMAL AS SEEING YOUR FACE IN THE MIRROR.

0-19

You don't necessarily follow the crowd. And it doesn't look like the crowd follows you, either. You're comfortable with who you are. Looking for role models? You're on a roll. Trying to be trendy? You know what's new. They should rename you "Even Steven."

0   9

20-25

YOU'RE AS NORMAL AS SEEING YOUR FEET IN THE MIRROR.

You're yourself, sure. But sometimes you like to be someone else. Or at least act like it now and then. When it comes to trying something new, you take it as it comes. But if there's something you inherited that just doesn't fit (your name? your style?), you're more than willing to trade it in for something else. Now that's fashionable!

YOU'RE AS NORMAL AS SEEING YOUR FUTURE IN THE MIRROR.

It looks like you like change. A lot of it, sometimes. You can switch into a new fashion, or a different nickname, at the drop of a hat. A funky hat. Don't let people say that you bounce around like a ball. Life's short. Why keep things past their expiration date?

18

27

36

ARE YOU "NORMAL"?

FUN

FUN QUIZ

BE SURE TO KEEP
TRACK OF YOUR
ANSWERS!

1 WHAT'S YOUR FAVORITE KIND OF MOVIE?

- Action
- Cartoon
- Comedy
- Drama
- Documentary
- Foreign
- Horror
- Independent
- Science Fiction

2 DO YOU THINK READING TEXTS OR WEB POSTS IS THE SAME AS "READING"?

- Yes
- No

3 GOT A FAVORITE AMUSEMENT PARK?

- Universal Studios
- Six Flags
- SeaWorld
- Disney
- Another park

4 WHAT'S YOUR IDEAL SPRING VACATION ACTIVITY?

- Basking at the beach
- Mastering the mountains
- Relaxing at the relatives
- Sliding in the snow
- Thrills at the theme park
- None of the above

5 READ YOUR HOROSCOPE MUCH?
- Yes!
- Sometimes
- Are you kidding?

6 EVER SEEN A UFO?
- Yes
- No

7 TIME MACHINE! PICK A DESTINATION.
- Jurassic period
- Ancient Egypt
- The Renaissance
- Colonial times
- The 1960s
- No way! I'll stay in today!

8 WHICH BAND JOB IS THE BEST?
- Singer
- Guitar player
- Piano player
- Sax player
- Drummer
- Something different-er

9 PLAY AN INSTRUMENT?
- A brass instrument
- A string instrument
- A woodwind instrument
- The piano
- The drums
- No, no, no

10 WHAT'S YOUR FAVORITE INSTRUMENT?
- Flute
- Guitar
- Piano
- Trumpet
- Violin

1

WHAT'S YOUR FAVORITE
KIND OF MOVIE?
WHICH FLICK DO *YOU* PICK?

39% LAUGH AT A COMEDY.

14% are happily shocked by horror.

13% say action flicks make them jump up and down.

13% are drawn to cartoons.

9% get serious about dramas.

4% think science fiction is out of this world.

2% say documentaries are big news.

>1% made foreign or independent choices.

and 5% say some other kind of film pops their popcorn!

WEIRD-O-METER COMEDY, HORROR, ACTION, CARTOONS = 2, DRAMA = 3, ANYTHING ELSE = 4

2 IS READING TEXTS

OR WEB POSTS THE SAME AS "READING"?

3 out of 4 kids agree that reading texts, posts, and online comments isn't exactly *Moby Dick*. It's not even *Winnie-the-Pooh*.

OMG. Only 1 in 4 kids thinks "texts" and "textbooks" are equal.

WEIRD-O-METER NO = 1, YES = 4

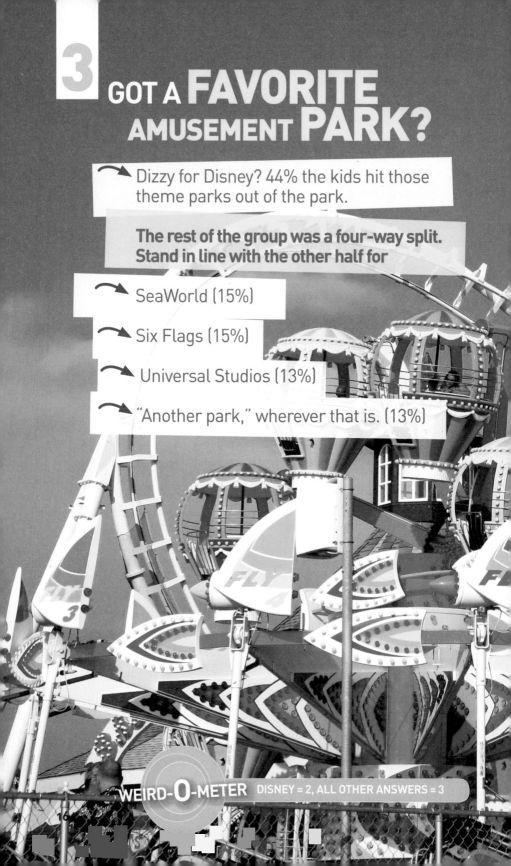

3 GOT A FAVORITE AMUSEMENT PARK?

Dizzy for Disney? 44% the kids hit those theme parks out of the park.

The rest of the group was a four-way split. Stand in line with the other half for

SeaWorld (15%)

Six Flags (15%)

Universal Studios (13%)

"Another park," wherever that is. (13%)

4 WHAT'S YOUR IDEAL SPRING VACATION ACTIVITY?

➤ When it comes to vacation, 41% kids would rather take a pass—an all-week pass at a theme park!

➤ According to 24% of kids, the next most normal dream trip is to the beach. No wonder Florida nearly sinks into the ocean every spring. It's all the visitors.

➤ A snow vacation hits the spot for 10% not ready to say goodbye to winter.

➤ 9% think a trip to see family is relatively normal.

➤ Last *and* least comes a trip to the mountains. The peaks may be high, but their popularity is not. Just 6% want to go.

➤ Another 10% say none of these vacations appeal to them.

WEIRD-O-METER THEME PARK AND BEACH = 2, SNOW = 3, ALL OTHER ANSWERS = 4

5

READ YOUR HOROSCOPE MUCH?

THE STARS PREDICT A NORMAL FUTURE AHEAD OF YOU.

Yes?
You and 30% of your friends have stars in your eyes and eyes on your horoscope, **you're normal.**

Sometimes?
The rest of the time you use your crystal ball with the other 35% of kids, **you're normal.**

Are you kidding?
Because it's hard for you and the other 35% to even believe in reality, **you're normal.**

Today is a good day to share *Are You "Normal"?* with a friend.

WEIRD-O-METER YES = 2, SOMETIMES = 2, NO WAY = 2

6 EVER SEEN A UFO?

→ **If you said no, you're normal (but not lucky).** 7 out of 10 kids only see UFOs in movies.

→ **If you said yes, you're lucky (but not normal).** 3 out of 10 kids say they've had firsthand experience, or first-eye experience . . . and lived to tell the tale!

WEIRD-O-METER NO = 2, YES = 3

7

TIME MACHINE!
PICK A DESTINATION.

GROOVY

30% OF TIME TRAVELERS DIDN'T WANT TO TRAVEL TOO FAR . . . JUST TO THE SWINGING 1960s.

If you wanted your mummy, you'd be like 14% of kids who'd prefer ancient Egypt.

Didst thou want to see the American Colonies? 11% of kids did too.

Perhaps visit Michelangelo and Raphael in the Renaissance before they were ninja turtles? Another 11% agree.

And dinosaurs didn't make many kids roar. Only 8% wanted to trek to find T-Rex. Probably because they knew that would be a short visit.

The biggest winner after the 1960s was the 2010s. A whopping 26% of kids don't even want to imagine a trip through time!

WEIRD-O-METER 1960s AND TODAY = 2, EGYPT, RENAISSANCE, AND COLONIAL = 3, JURASSIC = 4

8 WHICH BAND JOB IS THE BEST?

WHO'S ALL THE RAGE ON STAGE?

- 1 in 3 says being the singer would be sweet.

- 1 in 5 says being the guitarist would be great.

- 1 in 6 says being drummer would be bangin'.

- 1 in 8 wants to play piano in public.

- Only 1 in 20 wants to swing on stage with a sax.

- And the other 1 in 10 wants to play something different. Tambourines, anyone?

WEIRD-O-METER SINGER, GUITAR, AND DRUMS = 2, PIANO AND SOMETHING ELSE = 3, SAX = 4

9 PLAY AN INSTRUMENT?

- It's normal to say no. A third of kids don't play an instrument, but they sure can hit the "play" button.

- More than a quarter of the kids play piano, but hardly any of them can carry one.

- Strings struck a chord with 1 in 8.

- Woodwinds are wonderful for 1 in 8.

- 1 out of 12 kids has a drum set. Hopefully they *also* have ear plugs.

- Only 1 out of 20 kids plays a brass instrument. The rest of us don't have the lung power.

WEIRD-O-METER   NONE AND PIANO = 2, STRINGS AND WOODWIND = 3, DRUMS AND BRASS = 4

10 WHAT'S YOUR FAVORITE MUSICAL INSTRUMENT?

If you like guitars best, don't fret: more than 1 out of 3 kids names it as their favorite.

The next star is the piano. Over a quarter of the kids say it's their key instrument.

26%

38%

11%

12%

12%

Flute, trumpet, and violin play the same musical numbers differently, but they've got the same number of fans. About 1 out of 8 likes each of them.

WEIRD-O-METER GUITAR AND PIANO = 2, TRUMPET, VIOLIN, AND FLUTE = 3

WHERE ARE YOU ON THE WEIRD-O-METER?

ARE YOU NORMAL? ARE YOU WEIRD? ADD UP THE NUMBERS FOR **FUN.**

YOU'RE AS NORMAL AS AN ALL-DAY PASS AT A THEME PARK.

When your friends say "It's time for fun," they're singing your tune. But you don't let the fun get out of hand. After all, a barrel of monkeys is supposed to be big fun, but you're just as likely to notice the smell. That doesn't make you a party pooper—it just means you keep your head, except maybe after a sugary treat . . .

YOU'RE AS NORMAL AS A 5-DAY PASS AT A THEME PARK.

You push the envelope more than average. But what's in that envelope? A sudden party invitation? Enough DVDs for an all-night marathon? A fleet of rubber bands to launch at your friends? You have (some) limits and you (usually) know when to say "when," but sometimes you forget. Especially after a whole lot of sugar . . .

YOU'RE AS NORMAL AS OWNING A THEME PARK.

You're probably the kid who saw a UFO while playing the saxophone while dreaming of traveling to the time of dinos back in the prehistoric years. And if you're not exactly that kid, just the details are different. For you, fun is a quest, and you're definitely geared up for the challenge. All day. Every day.

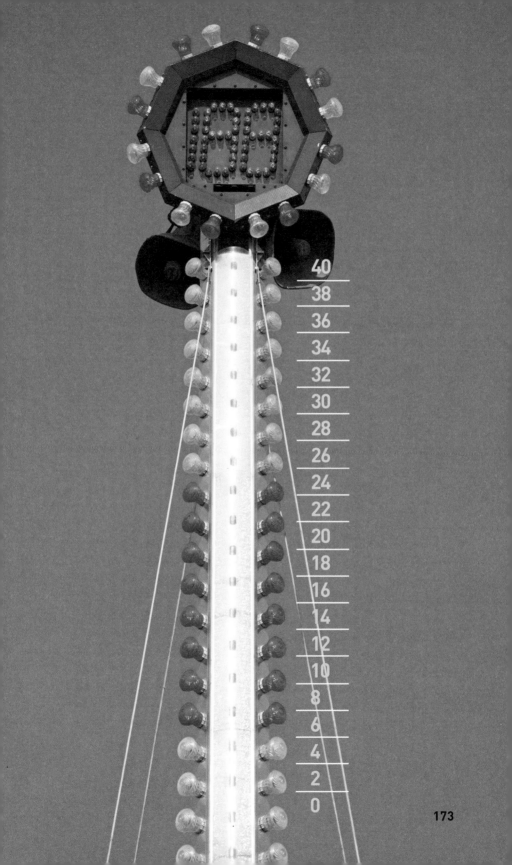

40
38
36
34
32
30
28
26
24
22
20
18
16
14
12
10
8
6
4
2
0

173

SOURCES

p. 16 www.americanpetproducts.org
p. 30 www.funkysnake.com
p. 49 www.playborhood.com
p. 85 www.kidsopinions.com
p. 106 www.scientificamerican.com
p. 119 http://vox.fastcompany.com
p. 120 www.timeforkids.com
p. 121 www.kaboose.com
p. 139 International Ice Cream Association
p. 148 www.care2.com

From the PBS Kids ZOOM Web Site, http://pbskids.org/zoom/index.html
pages 17, 18, 37, 38, 40, 51, 72, 73, 83, 89, 102, 123, 154, 167, 168, 169, 170

www.alfy.com
pages 19, 48, 52, 54, 66, 86, 100, 103, 116, 117, 118, 132, 136, 137, 149, 155, 166

National Geographic Kids' Online Poll, kids.nationalgeographic.com
pages 20, 22, 23, 24, 25, 39, 50, 53, 55, 56, 57, 162

National Geographic Kids' Panel Survey
pages 21, 98, 99, 101, 104, 105, 133, 134

www.ducksters.com
pages 33, 41, 150, 152, 153, 164, 165, 171

http://teacher.scholastic.com
pages 34, 35, 67, 75, 163

KIDS COUNT data center, datacenter.kidscount.org
pages 36, 68, 69, 70, 71, 74, 122

Kaiser Family Foundation, www.kff.org
pages 82, 88

Sports Illustrated for Kids, www.sikids.com
pages 84, 90, 91

www.factmonster.com
(c) 2000-2006 Pearson Education, publishing as Fact Monster
pages130, 131, 135, 138, 151

PHOTO CREDITS KEY GET = GETTY IMAGES, IS = ISTOCKPHOTO.COM, SS = SHUTTERSTOCK

COVER: (ROLLER COASTER), RACHEAL GRAZIAS/ SS; (PIZZA) SUPERSTOCK; (GUITAR), INGRAM/PREMIER EDITION; (PEANUT BUTTER) ARTVILLE; (DOG) DIGITAL VISION. BACK COVER: ALL ARTVILLE. 1 (TOP), SOUTHERN STOCK/ GET; 1 (BOTTOM), NICHOLAS EVELEIGH/ GET; 2 (TOP), 7HEAVEN/ SS; 2 (BOTTOM), LORI EPSTEIN/ NATIONALGEOGRAPHICSTOCK.COM; 5, ARTVILLE : 12-13, JOHNER/ GET; 14, KIRILL VOROBYEV/ SS; 15, JAMES STEIDL/ SS; 16, DIGITAL VISION; 17 (TOP LEFT), KIRILL VOROBYEV/ SS; 17 (TOP RIGHT), MARTIN RUEGNER/ RADIUS IMAGES; 17 (BOTTOM LEFT), ALEX STAROSELTSEV/ SS; 17 (BOTTOM RIGHT), RUSLAN KUDRIN/ SS; 19, LORI EPSTEIN/ NATIONALGEOGRAPHICSTOCK.COM; 20, YELLOW DOG PRODUCTIONS/ GET; 21, JAMES STEIDL/ SS; 22 (TOP), ANDREY ARMYAGOV/ SS; 22 (BOTTOM), DNY3D/ ALAMY; 24, MAKSYM BONDARCHUK/ IS; 25, ARCTOS/ SS; 26-27, NHTG/ SS SCHOOL: 28-29, IMAGE SOURCE/ GET; 30, IS; 31, HELDER ALMEIDA/ SS; 33, CHRIS CLINTON/ GET; 34, RED CHOPSTICKS/ GET; 35, TIMOTHY ARCHIBALD; 37, HELDER ALMEIDA/ SS; 38-39, ELNUR/ SS; 40, WILLEECOLE/ SS; 41, IS; 42-43, COSMA/ SS FRIENDS: 44-45, SS; 48, BRAND X/ GET; 49, FLICKR RF/ GET; 52 (TOP), ELENA ELISSEEVA/ SS; 52 (BOTTOM LEFT), GET; 52 (BOTTOM RIGHT), IS; 53, NEALE COUSLAND/ SS; 54, TIMOTHY BOOMER/ SS; 56, BRITT ERLANSON/ GET; 57, IGOR DUTINA/ SS; 58-59, EVA ABSHER FAMILY: 62 (INSET), EVA ABSHER; 62 (FRAME), IMAGE FARM INC.; 62-63 (INSET), VLADIMIR PISKUNOV/ IS; 62-63 (FRAME), IMAGE FARM INC.; 63 (INSET), BRAD WILSON/ GET; 63 (FRAME), IMAGE FARM INC.; 65, H. ARMSTRONG ROBERS/ CLASSICSTOCK/ THE IMAGE WORKS; 66, IMAGE SOURCE/ GET; 67 (TOP LEFT), INGRAM; 67 (TOP RIGHT), PAKHNYUSHCHA/ SS; 67 (BOTTOM), SERGET SKLEZNEV/ SS; 70, CWB/ SS; 70 (STAMP), IS; 72, 73, H. ARMSTRONG ROBERTS/ CLASSICSTOCK/ THE IMAGE WORKS; 74, LEW ROBERTSON/ BRAND X/ CORBIS; 76-77, ALEX KOSEV/ SS SPORTS: 78-79, SSGUY/ SS; 80, SERGEY SKLEZNEV/ SS; 81, CHARLES TAYLOR/ SS; 83, THE RF COLLECTION/ ALAMY; 84, PHOTOLIBRARY.COM; 85 (TOP), VERTES EDMOND MIHAI/ SS; 85 (A), VERTES EDMOND MIHAI/ SS; 85 (B), SERGEY SKLEZNEV/ SS; 85 (C), ALEX STAROSELTSEV/ SS; 85 (D), SUSAN SCHMITZ/ SS; 85 (E), CRAIG BARHORST/ SS; 85 (F), ALEXANDER ISHCHENKO/ SS; 85 (G), BENIS ARAPOVIC/ SS; 85 (H), MARK HERREID/ SS; 85 (I), D7INAMI7S/ SS; 85 (J), CHARLES TAYLOR/ SS; 85 (K), D7INAMI7S/ SS; 85 (L), NICHOLAS PICCILLO/ SS; 85 (M), MEXRIX/ SS; 85 (N), TRINACRIA PHOTO/ IS; 85 (O), ALEX POTEMKIN/ IS; 86-87, AFP/ GET; 89 (TOP), PAVEL SHCHEGOLEV/ SS; 89 (TOP LEFT), VERTES EDMOND MIHAI/ SS; 89 (TOP LEFT BACKGROUND), INACIO PIRES/ SS; 89 (TOP RIGHT), FFOOTER/ SS; 89 (BOTTOM LEFT), IS; 89 (BOTTOM RIGHT), FSTOCKFOTO/ SS; 89 (BOTTOM), CTATIANA/ SS; 90, IS; 91, IS; 92-93, GRANT FAINT/ GET BODY:94-95, REBECCA HALE, NGP; 97, FLICKR RF/ GET; 98, TOMAS LOUTOCKY/ SS; 99, IS; 100, FLICKR RF/ GET; 102, DMITRY MORGAN/ SS; 103, KURHAN/ SS; 104, SS; 105, CORBIS; 106-107, IS; 108-109, SEBASTIAN KAULITZKI/ SS. TECH:112-113, IS; 115 (BOTTOM LEFT), IS; 116 (TOP), IS; 116 (BOTTOM LEFT), IS; 116 (BOTTOM CENTER), TRISH/ SS; 116 (BOTTOM RIGHT), EVGENY KARANDAEV/ SS; 118, DMITRY MELNIKOV/ SS; 118 (INSET), SMART BOMB INTERACTIVE; 119, IS; 121, IS; 123, IS; 124-125, DABOOST/ SS. FOOD: 126-127, V. J. MATTHEW/ SS; 128, SUPERSTOCK; 129, GOODSHOOT; 130, SOUTHERN STOCK/ GET; 130, NICHOLAS EVELEIGH/ GET; 132 (TOP LEFT), DANNY E HOOKS/ SS; 132 (TOP RIGHT), SUPERSTOCK; 132 (BOTTOM LEFT), INGRAM; 132 (BOTTOM RIGHT), JOE BELANGER/ SS; 133, UGORENKOVALEKSANDR/ SS; 134-135, ARTVILLE; 136 (TOP LEFT), INGRAM; 136 (TOP RIGHT), INGRAM; 136 (RIGHT), GOODSHOOT; 136 (BOTTOM LEFT), GOODSHOOT; 138, OLIVIER LE QUEINEC/ SS; 139, MAREN CARUSO/ GET; 140-141, ARTVILLE. ME:144-145, IS; 146, HELGA ESTEB/ SS; 148, CAMERAMANNZ/ SS; 149, 7HEAVEN/ SS; 151, LANA K/ SS; 152 (TOP), TATJANA BRILA/ SS; 152 (TOP RIGHT), ALEX STAROSELTSEV/ SS; 152 (BOTTOM LEFT), VR PHOTOS/ SS; 152 (BOTTOM RIGHT), DJA65/ SS; 152, HELGA ESTEB/ SS; 153, RICHARD DRURY/ GET; 154 (TOP), IMAGE IDEAS/JUPITER IMAGES; 154 (BOTTOM), SERGEY MELNIKOV/ SS. FUN: 158-159, TOM BOL/ GET; 161, ZIMMYTWS/ SS; 162, STEVE CUKROV/ SS; 164-165, RACHEAL GRAZIAS/ SS; 166, FOTOLINE/ SS; 166 (BACKGROUND), PICTUREQUEST; 167, WATCHTHEWORLD/ SS; 168, ZIMMYTWS/ SS; 169, GINO SANTA MARIA/ SS; 171 (TOP LEFT), ELNUR/ SS; 171 (TOP RIGHT), BEDRIN ALEKSANDR/ SS; 171 (BOTTOM RIGHT), DM CHERRY/ SS; 171 (BOTTOM CENTER), HORATIU BOTA/ SS; 171 (BOTTOM RIGHT), LEBEDINSKI VLADISLAV/ SS; 173, EYEIDEA/ SS

FOR
HANNAH AND
SOLOMON
— WHO ARE NORMALLY
WONDERFUL.

I WOULD LIKE TO THANK MY OFF-THE-CHARTS AMAZING TEAM AT NATIONAL GEOGRAPHIC:

R.B. (Remarkably Brilliant Rebecca Baines),

E.A. (Exceptional Artist Eva Absher),

L.E. (Librarian Extraordinaire Lori Epstein),

J.E. (Joyful Editor Jennifer Emmett),

N.F. (Nationally Famous Nancy Feresten) and

M.B. (Master Bookmaker Melina Bellows).

6 out of 6 of you made this book possible,

only **1 in 10** jokes were cut,

and the result has been **100% fun.**

Special thanks to the students and teachers at PS 234 (New York, NY), Windermere Boulevard Elementary School (Amherst, NY), Robert Louis Stevenson Elementary School (San Fransico, CA), and Pioneer Middle School (Plymouth, MI).
                              —Mark Shulman